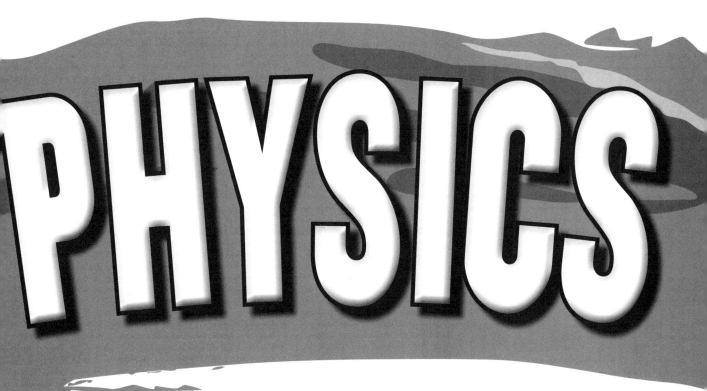

PHYSICS

INVESTIGATE THE MECHANICS OF NATURE

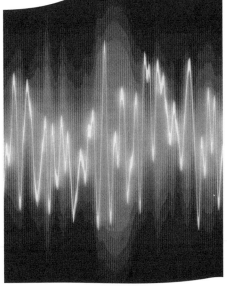

Jane Gardner
Illustrated by Samuel Carbaugh

green press INITIATIVE

Nomad Press is committed to preserving ancient forests and natural resources. We elected to print *Physics: Investigate the Mechanics of Nature* on Thor PCW containing 30% post consumer waste.

Nomad Press made this paper choice because our printer, Sheridan Books, is a member of Green Press Initiative, a nonprofit program dedicated to supporting authors, publishers, and suppliers in their efforts to reduce their use of fiber obtained from endangered forests.

For more information, visit www.greenpressinitiative.org.

This book was manufactured by Sheridan Books, Ann Arbor, MI USA.
July 2014, Job #360301
ISBN: 978-1-61930-227-3

Illustrations by Samuel Carbaugh
Educational Consultant, Marla Conn

Questions regarding the ordering of this book should be addressed to
Nomad Press
2456 Christian St.
White River Junction, VT 05001
www.nomadpress.net

~ Titles in the *Inquire and Investigate* Series ~

Contents

Glossary ▾ **Resources** ▾ **Index**

Timeline ▶

Third Century BCE .... Greek astronomer Aristarchus suggests that the sun is the center of the solar system.

1512 .... Nicholas Copernicus presents his heliocentric theory.

1595 .... Galileo Galilei sets up an inclined plane and rolls balls down it to show properties of constant acceleration.

1600 .... William Gilbert, an English physicist, is the first to describe the earth's magnetic field, though the Chinese had been using compasses for nearly 1,000 years already.

1609 .... Galileo builds his first telescope.

1613 .... Galileo describes the idea of inertia.

1621 .... Willebrord Snell presents his law of refraction.

1668 .... Law of conservation of momentum is presented by John Wallis.

1687 .... Isaac Newton develops his laws of motion.

1705 .... Edmond Halley predicts the timing and orbit of Halley's comet.

1752 .... Benjamin Franklin demonstrates that lightning is electricity.

1792 .... Antoine Lavoisier discovers the law of conservation of mass.

1798 .... Count Rumford suggests that heat is a form of energy.

1800 .... The electric battery is invented by Alessandro Volta.

1801 .... Thomas Young shows that light is made of waves and suggests the idea of interference.

1826 .... Georg Ohm presents his law of electrical resistance.

1848 .... Lord Kelvin theorizes about the absolute zero point of temperature.

1888 .... Heinrich Hertz discovers radio waves.

1895 .... Wilhelm Conrad Rontgen discovers x-rays.

1986 .... Antoine Becquerel discovers that the element of uranium is radioactive.

1897 .... Joseph John Thomson, a researcher from Britain, discovers the electron.

1898 .... Marie Curie discovers radioactivity with her studies of the mineral polonium.

1900 .... Max Planck comes up with the quantum theory of energy. His research leads him to believe that radiation is absorbed and emitted in discrete amounts of energy.

1903............ The first design of a spacecraft, including a multi-stage rocket, is made by Konstantin Eduardovich Tsiolkovsky of Russia.

1905............ Albert Einstein publishes his ideas about light and the universe in his special theory of relativity. He explains that nothing moves faster than light and gives us the equation $E = mc^2$.

1911............ Ernest Rutherford discovers the nucleus of atoms and creates the nuclear model.

1915............ Albert Einstein revises and updates his special theory of relativity to include a description and explanation of gravity.

1926–1928... John Baird sends the first television image of a series of moving objects. These images are sent across the Atlantic Ocean.

1920s.......... Edwin Hubble's research points to, and eventually confirms, that the universe is expanding.

1932............ James Chadwick discovers the neutron.

1930s.......... Plastic is developed.

1958............ Charles Townes invents the laser.

1967............ Pulsars are discovered, and by 1969 are shown to be rapidly rotating neutron stars.

1989............ NASA launches the Cosmic Background Explorer. This satellite is able to map microwave background radiation for the whole universe from our location in the Milky Way.

1990............ The Hubble Space Telescope enters orbit around the earth.

1994............ New techniques for sequencing DNA are developed, including the use of lasers.

1997............ NASA delivers the *Sojourner*, a wheeled vehicle, to the surface of Mars.

1999............ Scientists take a step closer to understanding human intelligence by simulating neural networks on computer chips.

2000............ Scientists believe that gravitational waves exist throughout the universe.

2010............ A team of astronomers makes the first direct measurement of the atmosphere of a planet outside our own solar system.

2011............ Scientists use black holes as a way to make accurate measurements of distances in the cosmos.

2012............ Researchers at CERN discover a Higgs-like particle at the Large Hadron Collider.

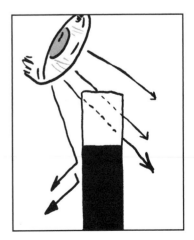

Introduction▶

What Is Physics?

Why is the science of
physics important?

✸ Physics is the study of the properties and interactions of matter and energy. Matter is anything that takes up space and has mass. Energy is the ability to do work.

KEY IDEA

Use the QR codes throughout this book as takeoff points for further exploration. When a QR code is provided, you can use a smartphone or tablet app to access the suggestion directly.

Do you have a younger sibling at home? Perhaps you volunteer in a kindergarten room or babysit for younger children. If so, you know that kids are full of questions. Why is the sky blue? Why doesn't the roller coaster fall off the track? Why does a fire truck make that noise? Why do the stars glimmer? How can I pull you in a wagon? The next time you are hit with these kinds of questions, you'll know that the answer can be found in physics.

Many people think of physics as a very complicated science with lots of formulas to memorize and diagrams to draw. Yes, there are mathematical formulas, such as

$$E = mc^2 \text{ and } F = ma$$

But memorizing a few formulas is a small price to pay for a deeper understanding of the world around you, isn't it? Pretty soon these formulas won't seem that strange or difficult.

WHAT IS PHYSICS?

If you consult a dictionary or a textbook, you will probably discover that physics is defined as the study of matter and energy and their interactions. And that's basically it! Physics is a part of almost every interaction we have with the world around us. While physics seeks answers to some very big, complicated questions in science, there is a practical and useful side to physics as well.

Understanding physics is essential to comprehending a lot of what goes on in our everyday lives. Computer technology, weather forecasting, medicine, and bridge and building design are all areas of study built on a foundation of physics. Physics can be theoretical and studied using computers, estimations, and probability. But it can also be hands-on and practical, using rulers, stopwatches, construction materials, and maps.

TRY IT OUT

The activities in *Physics: Investigate the Mechanics of Nature* will introduce you to the physics concepts that are used to explain interactions in nature and the world around you. Like physicists in a lab, you will learn to use these concepts to solve problems and explain events and phenomena. You will discover how physicists apply the properties of matter and energy to explain the world around them. Are you ready to use physics to explain how common things around you work?

⚛ There is a lot of new vocabulary in this book! Turn to the glossary in the back when you see a word you don't understand. Practice your new vocabulary in the VOCAB LAB activities in each chapter.

FROM THE GREEK WORD

The word *physics* is from a Greek word, *physis*, which is written φύσις in Ancient Greek. *Physis* means nature. Physics as a science originated in ancient Greece with philosophers such as Aristotle. At the time, philosophers sought to explain the world around them and to understand outer space. This was the beginning of what we now know as physics.

Chapter 1▶
Forces

What are forces
and how do they
work in the sport of
skateboarding?

BIG AIR

Tony Hawk was the first
skateboarder to complete
a 900-degree aerial spin in
1999. This involves spinning
two and half turns in the air
and landing in the opposite
direction he started from.
He really knows how to
make forces work for him!

Take a trip to the local skateboard park on a
Saturday afternoon and you are sure to see a lot
of activity. There will probably be beginners there,
cautiously rolling down some of the smaller, more
gradual ramps. And chances are there will be more
experienced skateboarders there too, performing
complicated and impressive tricks on the bigger,
steeper ramps.

Without even thinking about it, skateboarders
utilize forces, which are some of the fundamental
concepts of physics. If you can talk about
forces, then you can describe what happens when
someone is skateboarding. And you can use forces
to your advantage when trying out tricks at the
skateboard park!

SKATEBOARDS AND PHYSICS

Skateboard parks are built with the skateboarder, inline skater, and BMX rider in mind. They typically consist of ramps of different shapes, sizes, and angles, with rails where you can do more tricks. The ramps can be made of wood, plastic, sheet metal, concrete, or some combination of these materials.

Some skateboard tricks look like science fiction—the maneuvers seem to defy the earth's gravitational pull! But these tricks can all be explained with a discussion about forces. Force is more than just a push on the board, though. In order to accurately discuss force, it needs to be described in terms of strength and direction.

BALANCED OR UNBALANCED?

A skateboarder needs to be aware that forces do not work independently or in isolation. Forces might act in the same direction or in opposite directions. There are combined forces working together or against each other, creating what is known as a net force. The net force determines if an object will move and, if it does, in which direction.

The amount of a force is measured in newtons, which can be abbreviated as N. In a diagram, direction is typically shown with arrows that point in the direction of the force. A longer arrow represents a greater force than a shorter one.

Skateboarding is a great sport, as long as you are well prepared and careful. Be sure to always wear a helmet, knee pads, and elbow pads while skateboarding.

PHYSICS FACT

When a skateboarder pushes on the end of a skateboard, he or she is exerting a force on the board.

✺ **Unbalanced forces produce a nonzero net force. This changes the motion of an object.**

Forces may act in the same direction or in opposite directions. Consider the examples below.

When these two forces combine, a 16N force will move the object to the right.

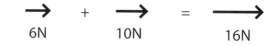

6N   +   10N   =   16N

But when these two forces combine, a 7N force will move the object to the right.

10N   +   3N   =   7N

These two are examples of unbalanced forces. When two unbalanced forces work on an object, the object moves. There is a change in the direction of the object.

But this object here won't move at all.

3N   +   3N   =   0N

The net force is 0N—the forces cancel each other out. This is known as a balanced force.

Balanced forces are not that exciting if you are trying to perfect your skateboard tricks. Perhaps your mom would rather have more balanced forces in your skateboarding bag of tricks, but it just isn't that much fun! Skateboarders want forces that are unbalanced. This is what allows them to stop, turn, and do many of the best tricks.

FRICTION

Friction can work against a skateboarder but can also be a skateboarder's best friend. Anyone who has used sandpaper or even just rubbed their hands together quickly has experienced friction. Friction is the force between two surfaces when they are in contact. In the case of a skateboarder, friction acts between the soles of the shoes and the surface of the skateboard, and between the ground and the sole of the shoe that's pushing off. It also works between the wheels and the ramp, and even between the skateboarder and the air!

What's the texture of the surface of a skateboard? It's rough or bumpy. This increases the friction between the soles of your shoes and the board itself. The type of surface has a lot to do with the strength of the friction. This is also why the ramps of a skateboard park are often made of a material with a smooth surface, as are the wheels of the skateboard. A smooth surface helps reduce friction, making the ride faster and more exciting.

One of the first tricks most skateboarders learn is the Ollie, which looks particularly impressive when done on flat ground. The skateboarder and the skateboard become airborne, without the use of hands! Mastering the Ollie is a good place to start, as it will teach you the basics for many other, more-advanced tricks.

⚛ **Friction is the force that resists motion between two objects in contact. It helps you stay on the skateboard. But too much friction between the wheels of your skateboard and the ramp will slow you down!**

PHYSICS OF THE OLLIE

What are the physics behind an Ollie? Watch one in action and you'll see how you can use forces and friction to perform tricks on a skateboard.

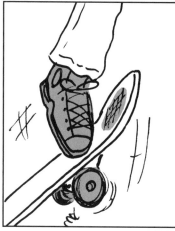

FLUID FRICTION

How can air be a fluid? A fluid is a substance that flows freely. It has no fixed shape and little resistance to outside stress. This is why both liquids and gases are fluids.

Standing on a thin board with four rolling wheels is not the easiest thing to do. The first thing you must learn is to make friction work for you.

Your body exerts a gravitational force downward on the skateboard and the skateboard exerts a force upward on you. The forces are balanced. There is friction at work here as well. Static friction exists between the board and your feet. This is the frictional force between two objects that are not in motion. When the board and your feet are not moving, an additional force is needed to get moving. And where would that force come from? Usually your foot.

Once the wheels on the skateboard start moving, they're under the influence of rolling friction. Since the wheels are rolling along a surface, the wheels and the material that make up the surface of the skateboard ramp become important. Sliding friction occurs when one object slides along another. This is evident when pushing a large, heavy box across a gym floor. You want to avoid sliding friction when skateboarding.

There is another type of friction that could affect your work on the Ollie. Fluid friction is involved when a solid object moves through a fluid. Are you skateboarding in the water? Of course not! Water is not the only fluid out there—air is also a fluid.

Fluid friction is more likely to be a factor in sports such as swimming, boating, or cycling. A cyclist zooming through fluid air is trying to go as fast as he can. His goal is to overcome the fluid friction that is slowing him down. The friction between the air and his helmet and clothing can add precious seconds to his time during a race. If you are traveling fast enough on a skateboard, fluid friction comes into play.

MOVE A HEAVY OBJECT

Inquire & Investigate

In October 2012, the space shuttle *Endeavor* retired from its duties in space. It was towed to the California Science Center by a pickup truck. You have been asked by a local elementary school to explain to a group of third-graders how it is possible for a space vehicle on a heavy trailer weighing a total of 292,000 pounds (132,449 kilograms) to be pulled by a much smaller pickup truck. Pulling a large object, such as a space shuttle, isn't easy but it is possible. Watch how it happened.

Ideas for Supplies ▼

- paper and pen
- poster board
- markers

- **What do you think the third-graders are going to ask you?** The best way to prepare for a talk such as this is to anticipate the questions: Was the truck a special truck? How could something so small pull something so big? Was there a really long rope or chain connecting the two?

- **To answer questions accurately, use language the younger students will understand.** What do you know about forces and friction? What do you know about surfaces?

- **One of the best ways to explain things to young students is to show them how this could happen.** What sort of diagrams could you bring to show them how this happens? You might want to include directional arrows, strength arrows, and force in your figure. What else is important?

To investigate more, prepare an example that allows you to demonstrate the same principles in the classroom. Common items such as a child's wagon or a sled could be used to show how forces and friction make the pulling of a large object easy.

Inquire & Investigate ▶

✻ The scientific method is the way that scientists ask questions and find answers. Keep a science journal to record your methods and observations during all the activities in this book.

Scientific Method Worksheet
Question: What are we trying to find out? What problem are we trying to solve?
Research: What do other people think?
Hypothesis: What do we think the answer will be?
Equipment: What supplies are we using?
Method: What procedure are we following?
Results: What happened and why?

SKATEBOARD RAMP DESIGN

Your town is looking to design a skateboard park and they have asked for suggestions. You and a group of your friends have some ideas for ramps and would like to submit them to the committee.

- **To decide on the size, shape, and angles of the ramps, take a look at some skateboard ramps, either online or at another park.** Some are relatively flat while others are quite steep with lips at the end. Think about what shapes would be good shapes for your ramps. What questions do you need to consider?

  - Who are the ramps intended for? Beginning skateboarders or more experienced ones?

  - How much room do you have at the end of each ramp?

  - How high can you make them?

- **Consider the materials you'll want to use.** One of the main ideas surrounding a skateboard ramp is the concept of rolling friction. You want to maintain a good ride, while being as safe as possible. What type of material should you use to coat your ramps? Research what ramps are made of today. Is this what you want to use for your ramps? Which materials are best for safety? Which are best for tricks? Do some materials wear away more easily than others? Are there other, manufactured materials that are safe for the environment and for the user?

- **What shapes do you want to utilize?** Skateboarders are concerned with the heights they can reach as they come up over the top of the ramp and the distances they can cover. Which shapes would work best to achieve the greatest height with the least amount of force? How do the forces on the person and the skateboard differ with different ramps?

To investigate more, work with your group to design a model of your ramps. Test them if you can with toy skateboards. Compare your group's design with the designs of others. Which would be the best ramp for experienced skateboarders? Which would be best for beginners?

Ideas for Supplies ▼

- graph paper
- pencil
- Internet

 **VOCAB LAB**

Write down what you think each word means: **force, net force, unbalanced force, balanced force, friction, static friction, rolling friction, sliding friction,** and **fluid friction.** Compare your definitions with those of your friends or classmates. Did you all come up with the same meanings? Turn to the text and glossary if you need help.

WELL, IT IS REALLY COOL LOOKING...

...AND SAFE, I HOPE.

BUILD A NEW SNEAKER

Quietly and under the cover of darkness, the ninja creeps along the wall. She leaps over a fence, lands perpendicular on the side of a building, and springs off to change direction as if her shoes were equipped with quick-release sticky stuff. Then she slips away like a cat, leaving no trace.

This reads like an adventure novel, doesn't it? What if you could make a sneaker that uses the power of friction to do amazing things? Try this activity—you never know what you might discover!

WHAT KIND OF FRICTION?

Static friction is the friction between two objects that are not in motion, such as your feet on the board. Sliding friction is when one object slides along another object, which might happen if you fall off your board and slide down the ramp. Rolling friction is the friction between a wheel and the surface it's rolling on. Fluid friction is the friction between an object and a fluid, such as a skateboarder moving through the air.

- **Decide on the purpose for your new and improved sneaker.** Are you making a sneaker that will help the elderly avoid slipping and falling? Will your sneaker be used to help rock climbers gain better grip with their feet? Will you market your sneakers to hall monitors at schools who do not want students to hear them sneaking up behind them? Will the sneaker be used by police to chase suspects through all sorts of terrain?

- **Design a prototype on paper.** What should your design include? You'll want to draw a diagram of the sneaker. Think about the frictional forces you are attempting to put to use with the material you'll use to retrofit the sneaker, and how your design will work.

- **Build and test your prototype.** Using materials similar to the ones listed or others that you think are appropriate, modify your sneaker so it uses frictional forces. Then test it. Does it work? What modifications would you make?

To investigate more, go online to research new technologies in sneakers and shoes for different groups of people. Sports teams, law enforcement, and the military all use specially designed footwear. What new advances have been made to work with or overcome friction? Prepare a presentation about these advances, including a discussion about your own creation.

Ideas for Supplies ▼

- pair of old sneakers
- piece of linoleum flooring
- sandpaper
- thin sheet of plastic
- large piece of plywood
- suction cups
- shellac
- hairspray
- corduroy cloth
- Velcro strips

Chapter 2▶
Motion

How do you know
if you are moving?

In two months, your town is holding a duathlon for middle school students. Each competitor will run 1 mile, bike 5 miles and then run 2 miles. With some training, you can probably do that! And it's for a good cause, to raise money to fight childhood leukemia.

On your first day of training, you have the strangest experience. You are on your bike at a stop sign and there is a large truck next to you. The truck starts to move forward but it feels as if you are moving backward. You need a point of reference to determine if you are actually in motion or not. A point of reference is something—an object or a spot—that you can look at and compare your distance to.

For example, if the distance between you and the stop sign on the corner is decreasing, then you are in motion with respect to the stop sign. It doesn't matter what the truck is doing. You may feel like you're moving when the truck moves, but in order to actually be in motion, the distance between you and the point of reference—the stop sign—needs to be changing. Motion is relative.

When training for a duathlon, one of the things you will be concerned with is speed, or how fast you are going. Your speed on a bike, or while running, is the distance you travel over a particular unit of time. To calculate speed, use the following equation:

$$\text{speed} = \frac{\text{distance}}{\text{time}}$$

You are probably familiar with the speed of a car. On most highways, cars are allowed to travel at a speed of 65 miles per hour (105 kilometers per hour). A car traveling at that speed will travel 65 miles (105 kilometers) in the span of one hour, or 60 minutes.

While training for the bike portion of the race, you may want to use a cyclometer. This is like a speedometer for your bike. It can give you your average speed and, with a touch of a button, provide you with your instantaneous speed at any given moment. The instantaneous speed is the speed you are traveling at a specific point in time.

CHOOSING A REFERENCE POINT

The surface of the earth is the most practical choice for a point of reference for motion on the earth's surface. Motion is relative—even though the earth is spinning, we don't feel it since we're part of that motion.

⚛ Speed is the distance an object travels in a unit of time. Velocity is the speed of an object in a particular direction.

WHEW! THAT HYDRANT IS A 10TH OF A MILE FROM MY HOUSE. I CAN USE IT TO TRACK MY SPEED.

Your average speed is the rate of speed traveled over the entire distance. For example, on one of your longer training rides, you travel 10 miles (16 kilometers) in 2 hours. Your average speed is calculated by dividing the total distance by the total time:

$$\frac{\text{average}}{\text{speed}} = \frac{\text{total distance}}{\text{total time}} = \frac{10 \text{ miles}}{2 \text{ hours}} = \frac{5 \text{ miles}}{\text{per hour}}$$

Another way to think about your motion is to consider your velocity. Velocity is speed in a particular direction. Suppose you start out on a training run traveling toward the east. You run for 20 minutes and then turn around and come straight home, running to the west. If your pace is about 6 miles per hour (9.65 kilometers per hour), your velocity is 6 miles per hour east on the first half of your run and 6 miles per hour west on the second half of your run.

After a few weeks of training, you start to wonder: Are you getting faster and stronger? Is your training making a difference? It's hard to tell. Then, in science class one day, your teacher introduces the idea of graphing motion. "This is it," you think to yourself. "This is something I can use in my training!"

That evening, after your bike ride and your run, you sit down to think about how to apply what you learned in class to your training. You were told that, motion can be displayed on a distance vs. time graph. You have your times and distances from each of your training sessions so setting up the graph is not difficult. Plotting time in minutes on the x-axis and distance in fractions of a mile on the y-axis, you can plot your run.

If you were running an average of one-tenth of a mile per minute, this is what the graph of your run would look like.

A useful thing about graphing your times like this is that you have a visual representation of your speed. The speed of your run is shown by the steepness, or slope, of the line. You can actually calculate your speed from the graph. The formula for the slope of a line is:

$$\text{slope} = \frac{\text{rise}}{\text{run}}$$

EXTREME RUNNING

Runners compete in marathons in all sorts of challenging places, such as on the Great Wall of China, over the ice at Antarctica, through an abandoned sand mine in Missouri, and along the base of Mount Everest. How does the terrain affect the different kinds of friction the runners will experience? How will it affect their speed?

Choose two points on the graph, say point 3 (3 minutes, three-tenths of a mile) and point 5 (5 minutes, five-tenths of a mile). The rise is the difference between the two points on the y-axis, and the run is the difference between the two points on the x-axis.

Your speed during this run was 0.1 mile or one-tenth of a mile every minute.

If your speed had been faster, the slope of the line would have been steeper. If you had taken a rest for a few minutes, the slope of the line would have been zero and it would appear on the graph as a flat line.

With these tools, you are able to see your progress. Not only does it make the training more fun, but you get to use something you learned in school in a real situation. How cool is that?

ACCELERATION

One thing you need to work on as race day nears is how to tackle the start of the race and how to handle the transitions from the running to the biking to the running parts of the race. When you focus on these aspects of the duathlon, you can see how it all depends on acceleration.

Acceleration is the rate of change of the velocity of motion. In other words, acceleration can be described as an increase in speed, a decrease in speed, or a change in direction.

Do you already have a definition of the word acceleration in mind? Typically, we hear the word acceleration used to describe something that is speeding up. In physics, the definition is a little different. When you mount your bike on the day of the race, put your feet on the pedals, and cross the start line, then you have accelerated. Your speed increases from 0 to something more than that. As you gain speed and begin to travel at your race pace, you have accelerated again. And you will accelerate again as you fly down your first hill!

However, the climb up the other side of the hill will slow you down. You are still experiencing acceleration—only this is a negative acceleration, or deceleration. Your velocity has changed—you have slowed down. You experience acceleration again when you round a corner without changing speed at all. As you move over the racecourse, you will probably accelerate and decelerate many times. And the final deceleration? When you stop on the other side of the finish line! Congratulations!

SLOPE SONG

Sometimes teachers work extra hard to get their students to remember things. Watch this middle school educator use his singing skills to teach slope, velocity, and acceleration.

DOG TRICKS

Have you ever seen one of those obstacle courses for dogs? The dogs jump over little fences and run around in rings. Did you ever think about how many times the dogs need to change direction, speed up, or slow down? Do you think the dogs realize that they are in the middle of a physics demonstration? Probably not, but in this activity you will have the opportunity to think of it that way.

- **Map out the obstacle course.** Create a design of your obstacle course on paper. How can you make the course easily followed by a dog and its owner? What can you include in your course? Small jumps, areas where the runner needs to change direction, areas where it will be easy for the runner to go faster and areas where they will need to go slower, and obstacles to run through or around will make your course interesting and fun.

- **Set up your course in an open yard, gymnasium, or other appropriate area.** Be sure to measure the distances between the different parts of your course and record them on the map. Do the runners know where they are supposed to go? How are they supposed to follow the path?

- **Try running the course yourself.** Then have other people or a dog with its owner run it. Use a timer to time them. What do you notice about your course? You might consider having people help you time different portions of the route. If necessary, ask the runners to repeat the course.

- **Graph the motion.** Fill in on your map the time it takes runners to complete each portion of the course. Choose small parts of the course and create time vs. distance graphs showing their motion.

To investigate more, challenge the runner to complete the course in the opposite direction. Graph the motion along the same portion of the course. How can you explain any changes you see in the slope of the line? How can you change the course to make it more interesting and fun?

Ideas for Supplies ▼

- large open yard
- hula hoops
- traffic cones
- small barriers
- graph paper
- unlined paper
- timer
- ruler
- pencil

AS SLOW AS MOLASSES

Have you heard the expression, "You are as slow as molasses in January?" It means you are moving pretty slowly. Molasses is a very thick substance that flows very slowly, especially when it is cold. But just how slow can it go? And what factors can make it speed up, other than changing the temperature?

- **To prepare your experiment, measure off a distance along the face of the paper plate.** Which variable are you going to change? What do you think will happen to the speed of the molasses if you use just a little bit of molasses? What if you use a lot? What if the angle of the paper plate is flat? What if it is tipped? How fast will the molasses move over 3 inches? Over 12 inches?

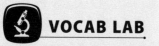 **VOCAB LAB**

Write down what you think each word means: **point of reference, stationary, instantaneous speed, average speed, velocity, slope, acceleration,** and **negative acceleration.** Compare your definitions with those of your friends or classmates. Did you all come up with the same meanings? Turn to the text and glossary if you need help.

Your graph might look something like this:

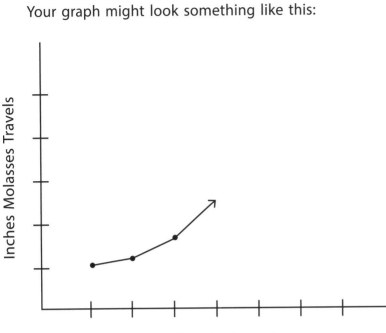

Inches Molasses Travels

Time in Seconds

Ideas for Supplies ▼

- molasses
- honey
- paper plates
- tablespoon
- ruler
- blocks or books
- timer
- microwave

- **Make a plan to measure the speed of the molasses.** Remember that speed is equal to the distance that the molasses travels divided by the amount of time it takes for the molasses to travel that distance. Start a scientific method worksheet to organize your questions and record your data. This is how you can calculate the speed of the molasses.

- **Look at it go! Run the experiment.** What happens? What is the speed of the molasses? How do you think you could make it go faster or slower? Try lots of different scenarios and record your observations.

To investigate more, microwave the molasses for several seconds to make it runnier. What differences do you see in the speed of the molasses now? What conclusion can you draw about the speed of molasses in January vs. the speed of molasses in August?

THIS SHOULD BE A SPORT!

HELPING OTHERS

Your neighbor breaks his leg in several places on a ski trip. He will be in a wheelchair for at least a month. You and your friends decide to help out by building a ramp to make it easier for him to get in and out of his house.

- **Your neighbor's home has a set of four stairs in front of the door.** With your meter stick, measure the height of the stairs. Record this distance in your notebook. This is the height of your ramp.

- **You now have to consider several other factors:**
  - what should the length of the ramp be?
  - how difficult is it to push or roll the wheelchair up an incline?
  - how quickly will the wheelchair roll backward if someone lets go?

- **Design a ramp that will keep your neighbor safe and allow him to get into his house with minimal effort.** Include measurements such as length, height, and the angle of the incline on your drawing.

- **Build and test your ramp.** Set up a data table with the relevant information:
  - angle of the ramp
  - length of the ramp
  - time for the wheelchair to roll down the ramp
  - average speed of the wheelchair, should someone let go of it

- **Run several trials to see if your ramp works.** Do you think it would be safe for a person in a wheelchair to use?

To investigate more, look at different ramps in your town. There are probably ramps in your school, apartment building, or other public areas. Use the same materials to test the speed of an object down those ramps. How do they compare to the speed of an object rolling down your ramp?

Ideas for Supplies ▼

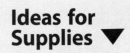

- flat board
- rollerskate or skate board
- meter stick
- protractor
- tape
- cardboard
- books or blocks
- stopwatch

Chapter 3 ▶
Newton's Laws

What happens when two or more things collide?

The physical interactions between two or more objects can be explained and described using Newton's laws of motion.

There has been an accident on the Old Eastern Railway. A freight train jumped the tracks and boxcars are everywhere. Luckily, the train was carrying lumber, not people, but the mess is tremendous. The accident reconstruction team is at the scene to figure out what caused the accident.

The engine is lying on its side, boxcars are piled on top of each other, and lumber has landed along both sides of the track. The engineer is standing to the side, scratching his head. The accident reconstruction team decides to deconstruct the accident one car at a time to determine what happened. What are some possible reasons for the train wreck?

NEWTON'S FIRST LAW OF MOTION

Before the accident, the engine was moving at a constant speed of 55 miles per hour (89 kilometers per hour) in a particular direction, in this case to the northeast. This means the train was traveling with a velocity of 55 miles per hour NE. The engine was on a track and would have kept going at that velocity for another 100 miles with the help of the engineer and the coal to power the engine.

"This train had some serious inertia," says the leader of the accident reconstruction team. "There must have been a tremendous force to change its velocity."

The rest of the team responds with blank looks on their faces, so the leader explains. "The train engine had inertia. That means it would naturally resist a change in its motion. As Sir Isaac Newton was known to say, 'An object at rest tends to stay at rest, while an object in motion tends to stay in motion, unless it is acted upon by an outside force.'

"The train was traveling at a constant velocity of 55 miles per hour northeast, velocity being the speed of an object in a particular direction. It would have stayed on this track for a long time if something hadn't knocked it off. What force changed its velocity?"

The team needs to keep another fact about inertia in mind. The more mass an object has, the greater its inertia, and the greater the force needed to disrupt its motion. On average, a train engine might weigh 200 tons. Because of its weight, this train engine has a lot of inertia and it would take a mighty big force to disrupt its motion.

PLANNING AHEAD

Watch a series of planned train wrecks and see physics in action.

PHYSICS FACT

Inertia is the tendency of an object to resist a change in motion. An object in motion tends to stay in motion and an object at rest tends to stay at rest.

NEWTON'S SECOND LAW

The team examining the track sends out a cry. The members may have found the cause of the accident! The other members of the team rush back to the tracks. A portion of one of the rails has buckled up. Was this the cause of the wreck? Could this displacement of the track derail a train of this size? Time to use physics to find out!

A BIRD'S EYE VIEW MAY GIVE US SOME CLUES ABOUT WHAT HAPPENED.

NOT ALL OF THE CARS DERAILED. DID SOMETHING HAPPEN FARTHER FORWARD?

NEWTONS

Remember forces are measured in newtons, which is abbreviated with the letter N. If you were to pick up a tennis ball or a lemon or a cell phone, you need to exert about 1N of force!

The second law of motion refers to acceleration, a measure of the rate of change in the velocity of an object. The acceleration of the train changed very quickly as the velocity of the train suddenly and dramatically decreased.

Specifically, Newton's second law of motion states, "Accelerating depends on the mass of the object and the net force acting on that object." Newton's second law of motion is represented by the formula $F = ma$. That is, the net force on an object is equal to its mass multiplied by its acceleration.

The mass of the train is approximately 397,000 pounds (180,000 kilograms). The train was moving at a constant velocity when a force disrupted that motion. That disruptive force accelerated the train in a perpendicular direction at 0.5 m/s². Therefore, the force that acted on the train to derail it must have been 90,000N!

$$F = ma$$
$$90,000N = 180,000 \text{ kg} \times 0.5 \text{ m/s}^2$$

The team agrees that is a significant amount of force needed to derail the train. It looks as if that buckled track would have been enough to derail the train moving at that velocity. Mystery solved!

NEWTON'S THIRD LAW

How does a train traveling down a track turn into such a huge pile of rubble? The team leader says, "For every action, there is an opposite but equal reaction." He turns to the team and explains, "Newton had a third law of motion. When one object exerts a force on a second object, that second object exerts an equal force back, only in the opposite direction!"

Overlooking the wreck, the team surveys the rail cars. "When the engine hit that spot, the velocity dropped suddenly and dramatically, causing a chain reaction. For example, the blue car in back slammed into the red car in front of it—the action force. Then the red care exerted an equal force back, but in the opposite direction." The inertia of the blue car caused it to maintain its motion even though the red car in front of it had slowed down significantly.

These forces do not cancel each other out. They are acting on different objects. The red car is acting on the blue car and vice versa. If two objects traveling in opposite directions hit an object, such as a brick wall, then the forces would cancel.

An object with a great mass, such as a train, requires a strong force to change its velocity, just as it takes more muscle force to lift a 50-pound weight than it does to lift a 5-pound weight.

✸ **Newton's third law of motion states that for every action, there is an equal and opposite reaction.**

CONSERVATION OF MOMENTUM

Moving objects have momentum. Have you ever run down a hill and felt as if you couldn't stop? You had what is sometimes referred to as forward momentum. If you had tried to stop, your body would have still moved forward. An object's momentum is determined by its mass and velocity:

$$momentum = mass \times velocity$$

Generally speaking, the more momentum something has, the harder it is to stop. This is why a runaway train can be a particular problem!

Back at the scene of the train wreck, some people are still not exactly sure what happened. It is important to understand the law of conservation of momentum when deconstructing this accident. Under normal circumstances, without the influence of outside forces, the total momentum of interacting objects will not change. If all the cars were in motion at the time of the wreck, then this is what happened.

The team leader fishes two toy train cars from his backpack and sets up a section of track to create a model of the wreck.

"Let's say," he begins, "each of these toy cars weighs 1 kilogram. In this first case, they are each moving along the track. This one is moving with a velocity of 6 meters per second and this one is moving with a velocity of 4 meters per second. Overall, the momentum of both of them is 10 kg·m/s. If they collide, which they will do because the one in the back is moving faster, then the momentum of the one in back is transferred to the one in front. Now both cars are moving at velocities different than before. But the momentum is still 10 kg·m/s! The momentum has been conserved."

Someone in the group speaks up: "But that's not really what happened, is it? The car in front stopped and the other cars ran into it."

"Exactly!" says the leader. "Let's see what that looks like. Suppose this car is stopped on the track. And this one is moving toward it with a velocity of 3 meters per second. Each train still has a mass of 1 kilogram, and therefore, the total momentum of this scene is 3 kg·m/s. When the trains collide, all of the momentum is transferred. If the car was initially in motion and then stopped as a result of the collision, the velocity of the car in the back is reduced to 0 meters per second and the velocity of the other one is now 3 meters per second. The overall momentum of this system is still 3 kg·m/s. So again, momentum is conserved."

Another member of the group speaks up: "The train cars here were attached! What happens to the momentum if the objects are connected?"

The leader explains. "The car in front stopped. It came to a velocity of 0 meters per second after hitting the damaged portion of the track. Let's say the car behind it was traveling with a velocity of 8 meters per second. Because the cars were connected, the momentum is transferred from one to the other, but the cars will both move slower than the original velocity. To conserve momentum, they will both move with a velocity of 4 meters per second. The mass of the system has been doubled but the velocity has been cut in half—momentum was conserved."

It will take several weeks to clear away the debris, but now that engineers know what caused the wreck, they can take steps to check the rest of the track for damaged rails so it doesn't happen again.

THE PHYSICS OF ANGRY BIRDS

Have you ever played Angry Birds? When the bird crashes into the pigs' hideout, the wall of the hideout exerts an equal force back on the bird.

PHYSICS FACT

Newton, who was the first scientist to be buried at the famous Westminster Abbey in London, based a lot of his work in physics on discoveries made by Galileo before Newton was born. Scientists spend much of their time trying to prove or disprove theories developed by scientists of previous generations.

WHO'S TO BLAME?

When someone witnesses a car accident at a busy intersection, the police ask the eyewitness to describe what he or she saw happen. This account, along with the work of an accident reconstructionist, points the finger at the driver who was at fault.

- **Start by setting up a scenario.** Using two or three toy cars, set up an accident scene. Cars can be at a stop sign, traveling in the same or opposite directions, or on the opposite side of a road.

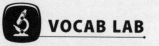

VOCAB LAB

Write down what you think each word means: **inertia, first law of motion, second law of motion, third law of motion, force, exert, conservation,** and **momentum.** Compare your definitions with those of your friends or classmates. Did you all come up with the same meanings? Turn to the text and glossary if you need help.

- two or three
  toy cars
- building blocks
- video camera
- ruler, pencil,
  paper

- **Choose one car to be at fault and create an accident.** Watch what happens as the car at fault runs into one or more cars. Replay the accident several times to be sure you know what is going on. Then use a video camera to record the accident. Watch it over again several times as you answer the questions that follow.

- **Map out the accident on paper.** Pay attention to details:

  - how were the speeds of the cars affected?

  - how were the directions of the cars affected?

  - how would the results be different if both cars were moving? If one was stationary? If the cars were moving faster?

- **Use arrows on your map to describe what happened.** Then, write a report stating why the car was at fault, using Newton's laws of motion and your diagram to explain.

To investigate more, prepare a witness statement based on physics. Using terms such as Newton's first law, velocity, acceleration, and conservation of momentum, write a descriptive paragraph explaining the cause and result of the accident.

HERE IT COMES!

HAMMER THROW SCIENCE

Have you ever been to a track and field meet? Did you watch the hammer throw? This is when someone spins around and around in a circle, with a heavy weight attached to a string. They let the string go and the weight goes flying. The person with the farthest throw wins!

CAUTION: It is very important to use caution when doing this activity. Do not stand too close to someone else. And hold tight to the string!

OLYMPIC MOMENTUM

Watch these Olympic athletes compete in the hammer throw. Notice how the athletes change the momentum of the hammer by applying force to it.

Ideas for Supplies ▼

- long string, about 3 meters in length
- small weights or washers
- meter stick
- timer

- **Make your own hammer.** Tie the washers onto the end of the string and measure the distance between the washers and where you will hold your hand. Record this distance in a table in your science journal.

- **Have a partner time your revolutions.** Stand with your feet apart and lift your hand up in the air. Begin to swing the string. Once it is going at a fairly constant rate, ask your partner to start the timer. They should count 10 revolutions and see how long that takes. Record this information in the data table.

- **Try it a different way. What changes when you alter some of the variables?**

  - The length of the string

  - The number of weights or washers

  - The number of revolutions

To investigate more, try releasing your hammer (taking care not to hit anyone) and see how far you can make it go. What affects the distance your hammer can travel? Can you make the hammer go as far with your weaker arm? Have a friend who is taller or shorter than you try it. Can they make it go farther? Why?

MOMENTUM DEFLECTED

Car crashes are caused by many different things, such as distracted drivers, bad weather, drunk driving, and turtles. Turtles? In 2013 in New Jersey, a driver slowed to avoid running over a turtle that was crossing the road. The car behind him struck the slowed car, crossed into the other lane and struck another car, which then hit a utility pole and smashed through a billboard. That's a lot of momentum deflected into different directions because of a turtle!

- computer access
- video camera
- pencil and paper
- toy cars
- dolls

BUCKLE UP!

Despite all the information supporting the use of seatbelts, some people still do not buckle up in the car. There are many public service announcements encouraging people to do so, but not everyone listens to them. Your job is to come up with a public service announcement based on science to show what happens when you don't wear a seatbelt.

Begin by watching several crash test dummy videos online. There are many videos that show crash test dummies with and without seatbelts.

- **Sketch out, frame by frame, an accident with a seatbelt (preferably a shoulder harness).** What happens to the vehicle? What happens to the object it strikes and the driver of the car? What happens in an accident without a seatbelt?

- **Add arrows and a step-by-step description of what is happening to the driver's body.** Can you explain what happened here using Newton's third law of motion and the conservation of momentum? Can you explain what happened to the car?

To investigate more, create your own video using toy cars and dolls to illustrate what happens. Again, frame by frame, walk the user through the effect to the car, the driver, and perhaps the object the car hit. Dub over your video to explain what happened and to encourage others to always wear their seatbelts. How does the speed of the car affect the severity of the crash? Does the size of the car and objects make a difference in the amount of damage?

Chapter 4 ▶
Gravity

Why does the earth orbit the sun and not the other way around?

⚛ Gravitational pull is determined by mass and distance. The gravitational forces between the sun and planets hold the planets in orbit.

10–9–8–7–6–5–4–3–2–1 Lift off! We have lift off of the space shuttle on its way to the International Space Station. Aboard is a team of five astronauts poised to conduct a series of experiments in space.

When sending astronauts and equipment into space, the first concern is for safety. But another important thing that NASA or another space agency needs to think about is gravity. Gravity is the attractive force that exists between objects that have mass. When trying to send a spaceship off of the earth's surface into orbit, the need to overcome gravity is vital.

Gravity is everywhere. If you are sitting in a chair right now, with this book resting on your desk, there is gravity at work. The chair has gravity and is pulling on your lower half, and you have gravity and are pulling on the chair. This book has gravity and is pulling on the desk, while the desk is pulling on the book.

The gravitational pull created by each and every massive object reaches throughout space. In fact, the gravitational pull created by your own mass reaches all the way to the edge of the universe! It's very weak, but it's there!

Gravity pulls things toward each other. It depends on two things—mass and distance. The earth's gravity is pulling objects toward it at a rate of 9.8 m/s². It's a good thing you are standing on the surface. If not, you'd find yourself falling pretty fast! And falling faster with each passing second, until the force of friction you experience from the atmosphere equals the force of gravity.

Mass is the amount of matter that makes up an object. You are made of matter, the sun is made of matter, and this book is made of matter. A spaceship has mass. This mass is significantly less than the mass of the earth. As a result, the earth has much more gravity than the spaceship. When astronauts blast into space, the gravitational pull of the earth is trying to keep the spaceship close to home. The spaceship has its own gravitational pull, which is acting on the earth. But it is too small to measure.

Take a look at the planets of our solar system—they are in orbit around the sun. That is because the sun is so massive, its gravitational pull can keep planets in orbit around it. The sun has a mass of 1.98892×10^{30} kilograms. This is roughly 99.86 percent of all the mass in the entire solar system!

Mercury, Venus, Earth, and Mars are the inner planets. Jupiter, Saturn, Uranus, and Neptune are the outer ones. The inner planets are smaller and rockier, while the outer ones are giant gas planets. The planets' positions in space are determined by several factors, including temperature and gravity.

GRAVITY IN THE SOLAR SYSTEM

The gravitational pull of the sun is 28 times greater than that of the earth! What about the gravity on the moon? It is one-sixth of that on the earth, which means it's easy to jump very high on the moon!

The gravitational pull of a planet will impact the weight of an object standing on that planet. The terms "weight" and "mass" are often confused. Remember, mass is the amount of matter in an object. Weight is a measurement of the amount of gravitational force pulling on an object. Astronauts on the moon, which has a gravitational pull of about one-sixth of the earth, will have the same mass as they do on the earth. However, their weight will be different. If an astronaut and all her gear weigh 690N on earth, then her weight on the moon would be about 114N. However, if her mass on earth is 155 pounds (70 kilograms), her mass on the moon would be . . . 155 pounds (70 kilograms)!

A WORD ABOUT PROJECTILE MOTION

Here is a quick assignment for you. Go outside, or into the gym, or try it in your classroom if your teacher lets you. What happens when you toss a ball up over your head? That's an easy question isn't it? It falls down—because of gravity.

Now throw that ball across the yard or gym (you probably shouldn't do this in the classroom). What happens? This answer isn't quite the same, is it? The ball seems to travel horizontally first and then gradually fall down. But the ball actually begins to fall immediately. The velocity of the ball in the downward direction starts at zero when you throw it horizontally, so it takes a moment for the ball to accelerate under gravity to a velocity our brains can notice. The ball will keep accelerating downward until it hits the ground.

Imagine you take a series of pictures of the ball as it travels in its path from your hands to the ground. It might look something like this:

See how the ball makes an arc? In physics the ball is called a projectile. A projectile is the object that is thrown. Its motion is called projectile motion. The ball is thrown with some force—you were trying to get it across the yard—but gravity takes over and pulls it toward the ground. There are many times when the projectile motion of an object must be considered—when a pitcher throws the ball across home plate, when a quarterback makes a pass, or when a tennis player hits the ball across the net.

THAT'S SO RELATIVE!

Are the laws of gravity the same everywhere? Even in deep space? In 1905, Einstein theorized that the laws of physics, including Newton's laws, were the same for any observer who was not accelerating. Einstein is famous for the equation $E = mc^2$, which states energy (E) is equal (=) to mass (m) times the speed of light (c) squared (2). This means that the energy content and the mass content in an object are directly proportional to each other. These ideas make up what is known as Einstein's theory of special relativity.

Einstein also wanted to address the idea of acceleration. In 1915, he published the Theory of General Relativity. This theory helped explain what he was looking for. Einstein theorized that massive objects—such as stars—create distortion in space. This distortion is felt as gravity.

For example, the light around a really massive object in space, such as a black hole, appears to bend. This is the gravitational pull of the massive object warping space and time, and therefore, redirecting the light. Closer to home, the orbit of Mercury, the planet closest to the sun, is changing ever so slightly. This is because of the impact the sun's gravity is having on space and time. In a few billion years, Mercury could be on a collision course with Earth!

SUPER-FAST

The speed of light, as calculated very precisely, is exactly 299,792,458 meters per second. That is 186,000 miles per second. Don't blink, you will definitely miss it!

TOYS IN SPACE

What sort of toys do you have in your home, classroom, or playground? Do you have a Slinky toy that can walk down stairs? A boomerang? A tetherball? Do you know how these toys work? Toys are usually adapted to the earth's gravitational pull in some way.

- **Choose a toy to take on your mission to the moon.** Look around your home, school, local park, or mall. What toy would you like to take with you to the moon? What things are important to consider when choosing a toy?

  - Is it small enough to fit on the spaceship?

  - Can you play with it alone or with just a few people?

  - Does it have many moving parts that might need to be replaced or repaired?

- **How does the toy work on the earth?** Does it depend on gravity? What must you do to operate the toy? Draw a detailed illustration of the toy and the way it works.

- **If you took the toy on the trip to the moon, what modifications should be made to the toy?** Do you need to change its mass? Add propellers? Provide a new source of energy?

To investigate more, create a marketing plan for your new, moon-friendly toy. Show the modifications that you made and demonstrate how it now works. Who might want to buy your toy? What will attract them to it?

Ideas for Supplies ▼

- several different types of toys
- pencil and paper

NO GRAVITY? NO PROBLEM!

Velcro uses hooks and loops to temporarily fasten things together. It's extremely helpful on board spaceships in zero gravity, when astronauts can't rely on gravity to keep their trays on their table or their chess pieces on the board.

I WONDER HOW WELL MY YOYO WOULD DO.

PROJECTILE MOTION

Imagine sitting at your desk doing your homework. You make a mistake on your math homework and, in frustration, you crumple up your paper and throw it toward the recycling bin. Surprisingly, it makes it in! Forget your math homework, now you have more important things to do! Pretty soon the floor around the recycling bin is littered with crumpled-up paper, but there are a fair number of papers inside the bin as well. This activity will help you improve your game!

VOCAB LAB

Write down what you think each word means: **gravitational pull, mass, orbit, dense, arc,** and **projectile motion.** Compare your definitions with those of your friends or classmates. Did you all come up with the same meanings? Turn to the text and glossary if you need help.

- **Set up your trials.** Pace off a distance between where you will stand to throw the tennis ball and the container you're aiming at. Start at a distance you think you can make pretty easily. Set up a procedure to follow. Will you vary the distance? Vary the height at which the ball is thrown? What combination of distance and height will ensure your success the most often?

- **Create a table in your science journal to record your trials.** You will need to gather data in a systematic way for this activity:

    - what is the distance between the thrower and the basket?

    - how long did it take for the ball to travel from your hand to the basket (or ground)?

    - did the ball hit its intended target?

    - how high was the ball thrown?

- **Toss that ball!** Use what you know about gravity and projectile motion and try for the most successful tosses. Be sure to accurately fill in your table.

> To investigate more, set up the video camera during a few of your trials. Examine the images in slow motion to see the projectile motion of the ball. Use the tape measure and the timestamp on the video to measure the approximate height and distance the ball travels. Use this information to graph the motion of the ball. How is this information useful to ballplayers? What would you have to do to keep your success rate up if you were playing this game on the moon?

Ideas for Supplies ▼

- tennis balls
- measuring tape
- timer
- small open basket or container
- graph paper
- notebook
- still camera or video camera

Ideas for Supplies ▼

- balance scale
- several common objects of different weights

A TRIP TO SPACE

Earth is very different from other planets in our solar system. On the moon and on other planets, the atmosphere is different than here on the earth, temperatures are much more extreme, and the number you would see on a scale is very different. Check out how much difference there is between the weight of objects here and the weight of objects on other planets and moons!

- **Choose several common objects that you might take with you on a space mission.** Try to find some objects that are large and some that are smaller. Need some ideas? How about a clipboard and pencil, a gallon of milk, or even a bowling ball.

- **Use a balance scale to measure the mass of each object.** Remember that weight and mass are not the same thing. Mass is measured in kilograms.

- **Create a chart in your science journal.** You want to include the name of the object, the weight of the object on earth, the mass of the object on earth, and its weight on the moon and on any other planets.

To investigate more, continue calculating the weight of each object on the other seven planets. Why do astronauts need to know how much their equipment will weigh on other planets?

Use the chart here to find weights on different planets.

Chapter 5 ▶
Electricity

Why does a light or
an electric guitar
come on when you flip
the power switch?

MS. INERTIA, WHY ARE WE AT A ROCK CONCERT?

ALL OF THIS WOULDN'T BE POSSIBLE WITHOUT THE PHYSICS OF ELECTRICITY.

THE LIGHTS, SOUND, AND INSTRUMENTS ALL NEED POWER TO ROCK!

⚛ Flowing electrons, in the form of an electric current, bring power to electric devices.

A musician is setting up his amplifiers, electric guitars, and lighting for a show the next day. He and his band will be using different circuits, switches, and batteries to run their equipment, providing the audience with the most dynamic show possible.

"Ouch," the musician mutters to himself. On this cold, dry January afternoon, he received a shock when he reached to plug in an amp. What exactly happened here, he wonders.

The answer is found in physics. All atoms are composed of protons, neutrons, and electrons. Protons and electrons have charges—protons are positively charged and electrons are negatively charged. Ever hear the expression "opposites attract?" Whether or not this actually applies to human friendships, it definitely applies to electric charges. A proton is attracted to an electron. But it's never attracted to another proton. Instead, protons always repel each other. Positive and negative charges attract, negative charges repel each other, and positive charges do, too. This is the basis of electricity.

An electric force refers to the amount of attraction or repulsion between electric charges. Electric charges, just like magnets, have fields around them. An electric field is the area around an object that is charged, where the electric force of the object is exerted on other objects that are charged.

The musician plugging in the amplifier experienced static electricity. Sometimes an object becomes charged. It ends up gaining or losing some electrons to give it an overall charge. This buildup of charges is called static electricity.

Have you ever walked across a carpet in your socks, touched something, and felt a shock? Static discharge is the loss of static electricity as an electric charge is transferred from one object to another. Electrons will transfer between a positively charged and a negatively charged object until both objects have the same charge. This static discharge often creates a spark. Watch a lightning storm from a safe spot inside. What you are seeing is a giant example of static discharge.

Charges are not created or destroyed. The law of conservation of charge says that if one object gives up electrons, then another object accepts them. Charges can be transferred in three different ways.

1. **Friction:** Have you ever rubbed an inflated balloon in your hair? At first the balloon is electrically neutral (the same number of protons and electrons). Rubbing it against your hair lets electrons onto the balloon and the balloon gains an overall negative charge. As the balloon gains electrons (giving it a net negative charge), your hair loses them (giving it a net positive charge). Now, if you hold the balloon away from your hair a little, the negative charges on the balloon will attract the positive charges on your hair. This also explains why socks stick to sweaters and sweatshirts sometimes when you take them out of the dryer.

CHARGED OBJECTS RELEASE THEIR ENERGY AS SPARKS!

ZAP!

CHARGES CAN CAUSE ATTRACTIONS. THE NEGATIVE CHARGE IN A BALLOON ATTRACTS POSITIVE HAIR!

2. **Conduction:** Conduction is the result of direct contact between two objects. Different objects vary in their abilities to conduct electricity.

3. **Induction:** Induction is the movement of electrons from one part of an object to another. It is the result of the electric field of a different object entirely. The two objects do not even have to touch to transfer the charge. This is why if you walk across a carpet in socks on a dry, winter day, you will get a shock before you even touch something metal. If your fingertip has a negative charge, then your negatively charged fingertip will induce a positive charge in the metal doorknob. The shock you feel is the electrostatic discharge.

You can't see electric charges because they are extremely tiny. But with the help of a device called an electroscope, electric charges can be detected.

When there is no net electric charge, the thin metal strips hang straight down. However, when some charged object touches the ball at the top, the charge travels either into or out of the thin metal strips, pushing them outward.

LIGHTNING

Mention the word static electricity, or just electricity, and most people don't immediately think of lightning. But lightning is actually large-scale static discharge.

Lightning is formed within huge clouds. These clouds are swirling and the water within them becomes charged. Positive charges move to the top of the cloud and negative charges move to the bottom of the cloud. Because opposite charges attract, the ground below the cloud becomes positively charged.

To lose that charge and become neutral again, the negative charges move toward areas of positive charges. The movement of electrons creates a spark, sometimes an enormous spark, and the result is lightning. Lightning may occur between clouds, within a single cloud, or between a cloud and the ground.

Advances in digital photography are allowing great strides in the study of lightning, but there is still much we don't know about this beautiful, dangerous phenomenon.

⚛ **A bolt of lightning is a very powerful, temporary example of static electricity. One bolt can measure up to 3 million volts and last less than a second. Temperatures inside the lightning bolt can reach 50,000 degrees Fahrenheit (27,760 degrees Celsius). Watch lightning strike from the ground up!**

ELECTRIC CURRENT

The Two Sides of Electricity

About 1,000 people in the United States die every year from accidental electrocution, usually electrical workers or carpenters on the job. But electricity can both kill and save lives. Defibrillators are machines that use an electric current to restart a heart that has stopped beating. They are used in hospitals, sports arenas, schools, office buildings, and other public places to help people who are suffering from cardiac arrest.

When plugging in the amplifiers, electric guitars, special lighting, and other equipment, musicians and their roadies need electricity. What they really need is access to an electric current. This is the steady and continuous flow of electrons through some sort of material.

Electric current is measured in amperes. This is abbreviated with either amp or A. It is named after Andre Marie Ampere, a French scientist and mathematician who is one of the 72 names engraved on the Eiffel Tower. Amperes measures the amount of electric charge flowing past a point in one second.

Electricity does not travel through all materials. That's a good thing! We'd be zapped by electricity all the time if it did. Some materials, such as metal, do allow electric currents to pass across the surface easily. These materials are called conductors, and they do a great job of transferring electric charge.

Insulators do not transfer electric charges well. These materials actually stop the flow of electric charges. Rubber, glass, sand, and wood are all good insulators. Check out the cord on any lamp, stereo, television, or microwave. You'll notice that the cord is surrounded by a rubber or plastic coating. This is to keep the electricity confined inside the cord. You're able to pick it up and move it around without getting zapped with electricity.

Have you noticed that water flows downhill? Electricity flows downhill too. Think of an electric circuit as a river with a current. A current of electricity is caused by voltage or potential difference. The difference in the electrical potential energy (voltage) is what causes the charges in an electrical circuit to flow—it causes an electric current. Another way to think of voltage is as the force that pushes the electric current.

Consider it this way. Suppose you have a plastic bottle with a small hole in the bottom. What happens if you insert a small flexible hose into the hole, secure it with clay, then fill the bottle halfway with water? If the end of the hose and the upper edge of the water are at the same height, then the water will not flow. There is no potential difference here. But if the bottle is raised or the hose is lowered, then the water will flow. That is because there is a potential difference. In fact, the greater the distance between the water level and the end of the hose, the faster the water will flow. The scenario is the same for the flow of electrons in an electric circuit!

ELECTRIC EELS

Electric eels can generate their own electric charge! Actually a type of fish, electric eels can generate up to 600 volts of electricity! They use this electricity to hunt, kill prey, and find their way around the muddy bottoms of the rivers they live in.

PHYSICS FACT

If you had a light bulb on the moon connected to a switch in your bedroom, it would take only 1.26 seconds for that bulb to light up 238,857 miles (384,403 kilometers) away.

RESISTANCE

On one trip back to the van to get extra drumsticks and guitar picks, the musician notices a small flock of birds sitting on a wire above the building. He knows that there is electricity running through the wire. In fact, he is using that electricity inside right now. So how, he wonders, is it possible for the birds to sit on the wire and not be affected at all?

The simple answer to that question is resistance. Resistance is another factor that affects the amount of current that flows through a circuit. Resistance, measured in ohms (Ω), describes how difficult or easy it is for charges to flow through a material. Resistance will slow down a current.

Resistance is impacted by four factors.

1. **The material of the wire.** Remember insulators and conductors? Wires made of insulating material will have a high amount of resistance, making it difficult for the current to move through it. Wires made of conductive materials hold their charges more loosely, so it is easier for the current to flow.

2. **The length of the wire.** The longer the wire, the more resistance it has.

3. **The diameter of a wire.** Thin wires have more resistance than thick wires. In a thin wire, more of the electric charges have contact with the sides of the wire, which slows them down. A thicker wire has a larger area through which more charges per second can pass.

4. **The temperature of the wire.** Cold atoms vibrate less, which makes it easier for charges to pass. Hot atoms vibrate more, which makes it harder for charges to travel. Resistance increases with an increase in temperature.

VOLTAGE SOURCES

There needs to be a source of voltage to create this potential difference within an electric circuit. Two voltage sources you are probably familiar with are batteries and generators. Each of these sources has two terminals. The voltage between those terminals is what makes the electrons move.

These factors are important, but still don't explain how the birds can sit on the wire without getting zapped by electricity. Electricity, just like many humans, takes what is known as the "path of least resistance." The electric charge, when faced with two possible paths, will take the easier one. So, those birds sitting on the electric wire actually offer more resistance than the wire itself. The electricity moves through the wire instead. Lucky birds!

WHAT ABOUT BATTERIES?

It would not be unusual for the musician and his group to have some batteries on hand for a backup supply of electricity. What if the electricity goes out during the show?

Batteries provide the voltage needed to get an electric current flowing. When you hear the word battery you are probably thinking of those small cylindrical or rectangular or coin-shaped things you put in flashlights, watches, and electronics.

In the physics world, even though those things are very useful to us, they are not true batteries. Cylindrical or coin-shaped "batteries" are simple cells.

Let's back up to the beginning. Electrochemical cells are special devices that change chemical energy into electrical energy. They are composed of two metals called electrodes, which are suspended in a substance called an electrolyte. Electrolytes are able to conduct electricity. Salt water is one example of an electrolyte. An electric field is set up between the electrodes and the electrolyte, and the voltage creates a current in a circuit.

What we think of as a battery is actually a simple cell. Typically in a simple cell, the electrolyte is a strong acid known as sulfuric acid. One electrode is made of the metal zinc, the other of copper. Part of the electrode sticks up above the surface of the electrolyte—this is called the terminal. This is where the simple cell is connected to the circuit. One terminal has a positive charge and the other side has a negative charge. A quick peek at any battery in a flashlight will show this with tiny + and - symbols.

A battery in physics—not on the shelves of your local hardware store—is a combination of two or more electrochemical cells in a series. In other words, the positive terminal of one electrochemical cell is connected to the negative terminal of the other one. Have you seen the way you have to stack the "batteries" in a flashlight in the correct way in order to get it to turn on? The positive end of one has to be hitting the positive end of the other. That is because you are stacking these single cells into one battery to complete the circuit!

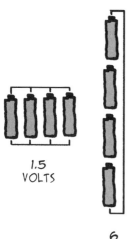

There are two types of electrochemical cells: wet and dry.

- Wet cells have a liquid electrolyte. Car batteries are wet cells, usually with sulfuric acid as the electrolyte.
- Dry cells have some sort of paste as the electrolyte. The A, AA, and D cell batteries that you are familiar with are examples of dry cells.

ELECTRIC CIRCUITS

You have just learned about voltage, current, and resistance. Now it is time to put them all together and flip the switch!

These three factors are related and can be summarized by Ohm's law. Ohm's law resulted from experiments by Georg Ohm in the 1800s. Ohms law says, "resistance is equal to the voltage divided by the current." In equation form it looks like this:

$$\text{resistance} = \frac{\text{voltage}}{\text{current}}$$

Or another way to look at it is:

$$\text{voltage} = \text{current} \times \text{resistance}$$

There are several ways to interpret or use these equations. For example, if the voltage remains constant and the resistance increases, then the current decreases. Or, if the voltage increases and resistance stays constant, then the current increases. Current and resistance are inversely proportional to each other.

ELECTRICITY INSIDE US

Have you ever seen an advertisement for a sports drink? If so, you'll know that sports drinks are a popular way to replace electrolytes after exercise. Our body's cells use electrolytes—including calcium, potassium, and sodium—to carry electric impulses across cell membranes. When we sweat, bleed, or vomit excessively, we lose those necessary electrolytes. A healthy diet of plenty of water, fruit, and vegetables will keep your body well equipped with all the electrolytes you need. Sports drinks are best saved for extreme circumstances.

All circuits are made up of the same features:

- an energy source, such as a battery;
- a resistor, which is something that transforms electrical energy (for example, a light bulb that transforms electrical energy into light); and
- a switch, which opens or closes the circuit.

These are represented by these symbols in diagrams.

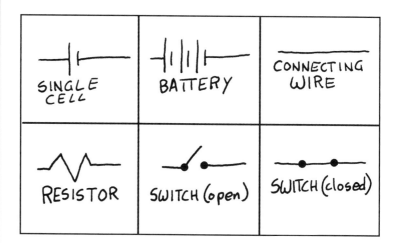

SERIES CIRCUITS

The band is almost ready to make some music. The stage is set and the instruments are plugged into their amps. The musicians are ready for one last run through before grabbing some dinner and a rest before the 8 pm show. The guitarists pick up their electric guitars and begin to play. Uh oh! One of the guitarists accidently disconnects her instrument from the amp and suddenly none of the guitars can be heard. What is going on?

The first thing our confused musician should do is check to see how the circuit that operates the guitars is arranged. The problem might be that they are all connected to a series circuit.

A series circuit is one in which there is only one path for the current to follow. The diagram to the left shows a series circuit. These three light bulbs are connected by a single wire. If one of the bulbs goes out, there is a break in the current. All the lights will go out.

There is another thing about series circuits that discourages many people from using them. Suppose three light bulbs are arranged in a series. If more light bulbs are added to the series, the light shining from the bulbs becomes dimmer. Remember that light bulbs act as resistors. Adding more light bulbs increases the overall resistance in the circuit. As the resistance increases, the current decreases, which means the lights burn less brightly.

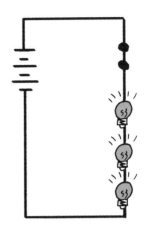

PARALLEL CIRCUITS

A parallel circuit is one in which the current takes one of several paths. The good thing about parallel circuits is that if one light bulb goes out, the others can stay on. A switch or two can be added to turn off some of the lights, but not all of them. This comes in very handy when wiring a home or setting up for a concert.

The issue of resistance in a parallel circuit is an important one as well. New parts of the parallel circuit can be added to expand it. When this happens, resistance decreases and the current has more potential paths to flow through, which decreases the resistance. This increases the current. The current is able to flow through the new parts of the circuit without impacting the original paths. As a result, the light bulbs do not dim when arranged in a parallel circuit.

LIGHTS ON!

Old-fashioned strands of holiday lights are on a series current, which is why if one bulb goes out, they all go out. This is a recurring joke in many holiday movies! These days, holiday lights are usually LED (light-emitting diode) lights, which last longer, use less energy, and don't rely on a series current.

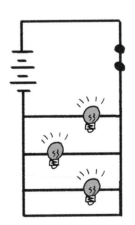

PHYSICS FACT

Current is measured with an ammeter. To measure the current in a circuit, the ammeter should be wired in a series circuit. Voltage is measured with a voltmeter. To measure the voltage of a device, wire the device and the voltmeter in a parallel circuit.

ELECTRICAL SAFETY

Before the concert can start, the equipment and set up must be reviewed by an electrical specialist from the fire department. If all goes well, then the band will be given a permit to operate the equipment and the concert may proceed as planned.

There are certain dangers that are prevalent when people come in contact with wires and electricity.

- Suppose someone touches a wire that has frayed. His or her body can form a circuit between the wire and the ground. This is a short circuit in which current takes the path of least resistance. The electricity flows through that person instead of through the wire. There is less resistance in the person and the current can be very strong. Short circuits can be fatal.

- You may have experienced an electric shock before. When an electric current from outside your body passes into your body, the shock may interfere with your heartbeat, breathing, or muscle movements. The severity of the shock depends on the current. If the current is less than 0.01 A, then you might not even notice it. Many of the shocks you get from walking across the carpet in your sock feet are a little stronger than that. But a current stronger than 0.2 A can burn you or even stop your heart.

There are safeguards in place to help protect people from accidental shocks and short circuits. Most contemporary buildings are built with a wire that connects all the electrical wires in the house with the ground. Not surprisingly, this is called a ground. A circuit is considered grounded if charges can flow from the appliances and wires in the house directly into the earth.

Take a minute and check out the electric plugs in your home. Many of them probably have what is known as a third prong.

Third prongs help provide a different path for electric current to travel through. There might be one on your toaster or microwave. The third prong connects metal pieces in the toaster to the ground wire in the building. If there happens to be a short circuit in the toaster, then the current will flow into the ground and not into the person toasting a bagel!

BATTERIES

The batteries you have at home are very corrosive. This means that the acid inside of them can destroy the materials it comes in contact with. But other, weaker acids can be used in batteries. What other substances can be used as electrolytes? Which ones are best?

- **Prepare the battery.** Cut 10 round pieces of aluminum foil the same size as a penny. Do the same thing with the paper towels. The aluminum foil will act as the source of the electric current you are creating. The paper towel will hold the electrolyte.

VOCAB LAB

Write down what you think each word means: **electrons, repulsion, amperes, conductors, insulators, voltage, resistance**, and **electrodes**. Compare your definitions with those of your friends or classmates. Did you all come up with the same meanings? Turn to the text and glossary if you need help.

- **Assemble your single cell battery.** Create a stack of pennies, paper towels, and aluminum foil by layering the items in this order over and over:

  - penny

  - paper towel

  - aluminum foil

  - paper towel

- **Carefully wrap the assembly in electrical tape—just be sure not to completely cover the whole thing.** The paper towel pieces should be in contact with the electrolyte.

- **Choose your electrolyte.** Which electrolyte do you think will work best? Consider using one of the following solutions, or one of your own:

  - lemon or lime juice
  - freshwater
  - salt water
  - soda
  - vinegar

- **Test the electrolyte.** Submerge your homemade battery into the electrolyte to soak the paper towels. Then remove the battery and connect the wires to the terminals of the battery. Connect one wire to the penny on one side and the other to the aluminum foil on the other end of the stack and attach with tape. Wrap the entire battery in electrical tape to reduce the chance of a short circuit. Set up the voltmeter to measure the strength of your battery and the electrolyte. Record and compare your results.

> To investigate more, attach a small light bulb to the wires. In a dark room, compare the brightness of a battery with one electrolyte versus the brightness of a battery with a different electrolyte. Which type of substance makes the best electrolyte for homemade batteries?

Ideas for Supplies ▼

- 10–20 copper pennies
- aluminum foil
- paper towels
- electrical tape
- lemon juice
- salt water
- soda
- vinegar
- fresh water
- wires
- voltmeter
- small light bulb

EUREKA!

IS THERE AN ELECTRIC CHARGE IN THE HOUSE?

How do you know if there are electric charges around? Find out in this investigation.

- **Begin by crumpling the aluminum foil.** Make a ball of crumpled-up aluminum foil from one piece. Make a smaller roll of aluminum foil that looks like a pencil. Attach the two together so that it resembles a lollipop.

- **Poke a hole in the lid.** Carefully punch a hole through the lid of the jar. Place the stick part of your aluminum foil lollipop through the hole, leaving the crumpled ball on top. Bend the stick part to form a hook.

- **Make your electroscope.** Fold a piece of aluminum foil in the middle and smooth it out so that it forms a long strip. Bend this in half and balance it over the hook. Carefully place the electroscope in the jar and screw the lid shut.

- **Do you observe any electric charges?** What happens if you:

  - move the electroscope near the microwave and cook some popcorn?

  - run a comb through your hair and then touch the comb to the ball?

  - rub a balloon on a wool sweater and then touch the balloon to the ball?

  - bring the electroscope near an electrical outlet?

To investigate more, use your electroscope on a dry day and later on a rainy day. Compare your results for both days. Why might it work differently on each day? Have your electroscope handy for when a lightning storm comes. Leave your device outside where you can see it from a window, so you can be safe. How does your electroscope react to a lightning storm?

Ideas for Supplies ▼

- aluminum foil
- glass jar with plastic lid
- hole punch or drill
- comb
- balloon

WOW! I DIDN'T EXPECT THE CAT TO BE THAT CHARGED!

MEOW

Ideas for Supplies ▼

- Styrofoam plate
- thumbtack
- pencil with eraser
- aluminum pie plate
- small piece of wood
- video camera

I AM THOR! GOD OF LIGHTNING AND THUNDER!

GRRL

MAKING LIGHTNING

We have all seen magnificent bolts of lightning streaking across the sky, accompanied by a bone-rattling, thunderous boom. It's like fireworks, only without the colors. But lightning is actually a pretty simple phenomenon. So simple that you can make it yourself!

NOTE: This activity will not work well on a humid day. It is best done on a dry day in the winter.

- **Set up the experiment.** Push the thumbtack through the bottom of the aluminum pie plate. Then place the pencil on the thumbtack by sticking the eraser on the point. Place the Styrofoam plate upside down on the table and rub the wool on the bottom of the plate. Rub hard and fast for one minute. Pick the pie plate up by the pencil handle and place it on top of the Styrofoam plate so the bottoms are touching. Touch the pie plate with your finger. What do you feel?

- **Try it with the lights out.** Repeat the steps in a dark room. What did you feel? What did you see?

- **Repeat again and videotape it.** Play the video in slow motion. Can you explain what you see?

To investigate more, obtain a neon tube from a scientific supply store. Hold the tube so that your finger is covering one end. Touch the other end of the tube to the pie plate and see what happens. What are you seeing? How is this possible?

Chapter 6▶
Magnetism

Why are some—but
not all—metal objects
attracted to magnets?

🔬 Materials with magnetic properties typically contain the element iron.

MAGLEV MAGIC

As of 2013 there are only two commercial maglev trains in operation—in China and Japan. Two more are under construction, one in South Korea and another in China. Watch videos of maglev trains in action.

Imagine sitting in a train speeding along a track. Now, imagine if that train were not actually on the track. What if it were hovering about one-half inch (10 millimeters) above the track and speeding along at rates of at least 300 miles per hour (483 kilometers per hour)? You might be riding a maglev train.

Maglev trains are built with magnets underneath them that lift them off the tracks to reduce friction. Maglev trains can travel at greater speeds than normal trains, and use less energy to operate. How do magnets do all this?

Magnets are not just those things with a north and south pole found in a compass. Magnets can be one of several types of material. The only requirement is that the material must produce a magnetic field.

Any magnet, no matter what the size, has two magnetic poles. These are called the north pole and the south pole, respectively. Remember the saying we discussed before when we talked about protons and electrons? Opposites attract—and the same goes for magnetic poles. The north pole of a magnet is always attracted to the south pole of a different magnet. This will draw the magnets toward each other. However, the north pole of a magnet will repel, or push away, the north pole of another magnet.

This attraction or repulsion between the poles of a magnet has a special name—magnetic force.

The maglev train operates on the basis of magnetic force. The poles of the magnets on the bottom of the train face in the same direction as the magnets in the tracks. This pushes the magnets apart, or repels them, so the train is lifted up.

MAGNETIC FIELDS OF DREAMS

Magnets have a field. Think of it as a force field. If you hold a bar magnet under a tray filled with metal shavings, or drop a magnet into a pile of metal filings, you'll be able to see the magnetic field around the magnet.

Maglev is short for magnetic levitation, which uses magnets to lift and propel trains along their tracks.

LED BY LODESTONE

Ancient Greeks were the first to describe the qualities of a magnet, which was also called lodestone. Later civilizations believed that entire islands were made of lodestone, and when ships disappeared at sea they blamed these magnetic islands for pulling the ships onto their rocky shores by using magnetism on the ships' iron nails.

⚛ People have projected superstitious qualities onto magnets since they were discovered. Magnets have been thought to be evil, harmful, healing, and magical at different times by different populations.

The actual magnetic lines are invisible, but they have an impact on the area surrounding the magnet. If arrows were drawn on these lines, it would be clear that the magnetic field lines always spread out from the north pole, curve in a loop around the magnet, and then extend into the south pole.

The closer the lines are, the stronger the field. Where on the magnet is the field the strongest? Where is it the weakest?

WHAT MAKES A MAGNET?

Why do the rails and the maglev train need to be built of metal rather than wood or plastic? To answer that question, you need to study the atom.

Atoms make up matter. If you have a chunk of pure iron, and are able to break it into smaller and smaller chunks, then the absolutely smallest chunk you could have that was still iron would be an atom. Atoms are the smallest parts of an element that still have the characteristics and properties of that element.

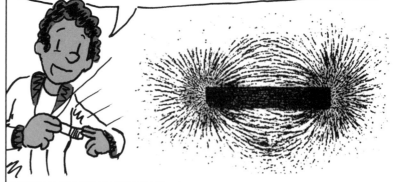

As of 2012, there were 118 known elements. Some are familiar to you. Oxygen, hydrogen, gold, silver, and neon are all elements on the periodic table. Others, such as flerovium, ununtrium, and ununoctium, are probably less well known. The first 98 elements occur in nature. Elements 99 to 118 are only produced in the laboratory. Each element, however, has a structure and composition that makes it unique from all other elements.

Each atom is made of the same parts. There is a nucleus at the center of the atom with a cloud of electrons circling around the nucleus. Inside the nucleus there may be two types of particles—protons and neutrons.

- Electrons carry a negative charge. They orbit around the nucleus.

- Protons carry a positive charge. They are found inside the nucleus.

- Neutrons carry no charge at all. These neutral parts of the atom also reside in the nucleus.

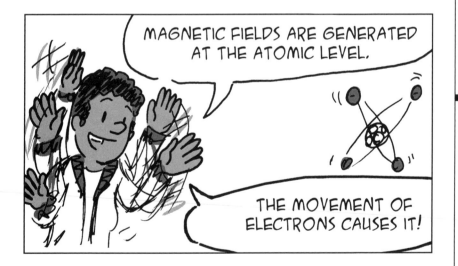

MAGNETIC FIELDS ARE GENERATED AT THE ATOMIC LEVEL.

THE MOVEMENT OF ELECTRONS CAUSES IT!

A Scottish scientist named James Clerk Maxwell established the relationship between magnetism and electricity in 1862, more than 30 years before the electron was even discovered.

MAKING MAGNETS

It's possible to change the alignment of the domains within a material. Depending upon the material, exposure to a magnet may help to align the domains. This will turn the material into a temporary magnet.

When talking about magnets, the most important part of the atom to understand is the movement of the electrons. These small particles have what is known as electron spin. They behave as if they were spinning on an axis while revolving around the nucleus of an atom. This spinning motion creates a magnetic field. The electrons then behave as if they were tiny magnets circling the nucleus. Usually, electrons spin around in pairs—pairs that spin in opposite directions. This means that the magnetic field produced by the electrons cancel, giving the overall atom a weak magnetic field. But some atoms have unpaired electrons. There is no cancellation of magnetic field and, in fact, the atoms have a stronger magnetic field.

Another important factor is the magnetic domain of atoms. Occasionally, the magnetic fields of a bunch of atoms of the same element line up with each other. This group of atoms now has its own magnetic field, referred to as a magnetic domain. As a whole, the magnetic domain acts as a magnet with north and south poles.

For clarification, magnetic fields of many atoms align to form a magnetic domain. This magnetic domain acts as one bar magnet, with a north and a south pole. It is a whole bunch of parts working together to form one thing.

In a material, if the domains are all, or nearly all, aligned in the same direction, then the material itself will be magnetized. If the domains point in random directions, the material is not magnetized.

ALL ABOUT MAGNETS

Nothing lasts forever. This applies to magnets as well. A magnet can be created, destroyed, and even broken.

While it is true that magnets exist in nature, those magnets on the refrigerator hanging up your spelling test, soccer schedule, or takeout menu from the pizza place down the street are manmade. They are made by placing some ferromagnetic material into a magnetic field or by rubbing a strong magnet on it.

Later in this chapter, you will have the opportunity to make your own magnet. But its magnetic properties will not last long. This is called a temporary magnet. The magnets made and sold in stores are called permanent magnets.

- cardboard
- wooden blocks
- bar magnets
- glue
- toy car or foam block

✸ Birds and insects use an inherent understanding of magnets when they migrate over the earth's surface and through its magnetic field.

MAKE YOUR OWN MAGLEV TRAIN

You can create your own maglev train right at home.

- **Set up a cardboard track for the toy car or foam block.** You should include sides on the track so the car doesn't fall off. Arrange bar magnets under the track. During setup, consider a few different things:
  - the direction the magnets are facing,
  - how far apart to space them, and
  - the alignment of the north and south poles.

- **Glue a bar magnet to the bottom of the car.** Which way will you glue the magnet to the car? Keep in mind what you know about magnets and poles.

- **All aboard!** Put your train on the track and give it a little nudge. What happens? Does the train travel down the track? You may need to adjust your setup if the train does not move. Can you make it go faster? What modifications might make that possible?

To investigate more, see if you can get your maglev train to go up a slight incline. Use building blocks to elevate a portion of your track slightly. Is it possible, with the addition of more magnets, to make the train go uphill? How does the number of magnets impact the behavior of the train?

VENDING MACHINE SECURITY

Have you ever been to an arcade or used a vending machine? Perhaps you ran out of change and couldn't play anymore. This doesn't always stop people. Sometimes people cheat the system and use slugs or fake coins to continue to snack or play games. In this activity you will have the opportunity to make sure that doesn't happen!

Ideas for Supplies ▼

- cardboard
- string
- steel washers
- tape
- magnets
- coins

- **Determine which of your materials are attracted to magnets and which aren't.** Use your magnet to test for magnetism. Record your observations in your scientific notebook.

- **Design a device that will separate the magnetic materials from the nonmagnetic materials.** What might you want to include in your design? Here are some options:

  - a track that will allow the coins or washers to pass in a straight line,

  - alternative paths for the items not attracted to the magnet, or

  - a series of magnets to attract any magnetic material that does pass through.

- **Test your device.** Does it work? Are you able to separate the magnetic washers from the nonmagnetic coins? How could you modify your device to make it even better?

> To investigate more, consider other ways people use magnets in daily life, from inside refrigerators to inside cars to inside a cow's stomach. How would our lives be different if we didn't have magnets?

MAGNET MAGIC

It is possible to turn a common, everyday object such as a paperclip into a magnet. A sewing company recently realized it spends thousands of dollars each year replacing the pins that fall on the floor. It has asked you and your classmates to design a magnetic device that can pick up as many pins as possible in a short period of time, without having to be "re-magnetized" very often. How many pins can you pick up?

VOCAB LAB

Write down what you think each word means: **magnetic force**, **magnetic domain**, **atom, electron, proton, neutron,** and **ferromagnetic material**. Compare your definitions with those of your friends or classmates. Did you all come up with the same meanings? Turn to the text and glossary if you need help.

- **Choose your materials.** What will you make your magnet out of? Remember that objects containing at least some iron, such as steel, are easiest to magnetize. You'll want to consider the size and composition of your device. How easy will it be to hold or manipulate your object? You may want to construct a handle out of tape to make it easier.

- **To make a magnet, use the bar magnet to rub your object repeatedly in the same direction.** Test it out. Does your new magnet pick up small metal objects such as pins or earring backs?

- **What factors should you take into consideration when making a magnet?** Compare three or four different materials. Keep a log comparing what you discover:

  - what is the object?

  - what is it made of?

  - how long and wide is the object?

  - how much does it weigh?

  - how long was it exposed to the bigger magnet?

  - how many pins can it pick up?

  - what is the length of time it takes for the magnet to become weaker?

> To investigate more, consider the shape of your homemade magnet. If the magnet is curved, will it pick up more pins than if it is straight? See if you can find a difference by creating some new magnets and testing them.

Ideas for Supplies ▼

- paper clips
- steel nails
- strong bar magnet
- masking tape
- small pins
- metal earring backs

Chapter 7 ▶
Light and Optics

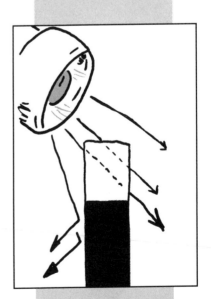

Why can light pass
through some
objects, but not all?

Do you ever feel like someone is watching you? Chances are, someone probably is. Not in a creepy sort of way, but in a security sort of way. Most large parking lots at malls, shopping areas, or even your school use cameras to monitor activities. Inside stores, single-sided mirrors, cameras, and other devices help deter shoplifters and keep customers and employees safe.

WINDOWS

Have you ever noticed how some windows are very clear and you can see through them? Other windows are cloudy, allowing only some light through. Many times this sort of glass is used for privacy or decoration at a shopping mall. Windows that are clear are transparent. They allow light to pass through without scattering it.

Those cloudy windows, which allow a little light through, can be described as being translucent. A translucent material scatters the light rays that pass through it. If someone was standing behind a translucent window, you would know someone was there, but it would be difficult to make out exactly who it was—he or she would look blurry and distorted.

Other objects are opaque—light does not pass through them at all. The light waves are either absorbed by the material or reflect off of it. Thick plastic sheeting can often be opaque, as can walls and flooring materials. Many objects are opaque.

COLOR

Walk around any mall and you'll be assaulted by movie posters, advertisements, and event flyers. The brightest and most colorful posters are the ones that draw your eyes.

One store is advertising a sale on brightly colored basketball sneakers. As a student of physics, you wonder why they look the way they do.

The color of an opaque object, such as those bright orange shoelaces, is the color that the object reflects. Visible light, the light that we see, usually appears as white, but it's actually a combination of many colors. Pass light through a prism and you will see a rainbow. Visible light is made up of red, orange, yellow, green, blue, indigo, and violet.

When light strikes these shoelaces, they absorb some wavelengths of the light and reflect others. They absorb red, yellow, green, blue, indigo, and violet, and reflect orange. The reflected orange light reaches your eyes, and your eyes and brain, working together, see the color orange.

 Light can pass completely through transparent objects and through translucent objects to a certain extent, but not through opaque objects.

PHYSICS FACT

Some people can't see all the colors. They may be colorblind from damage to their eyes or because they were born that way. Test your own color sight here.

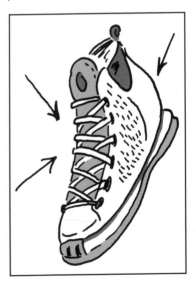

MIRROR, MIRROR

Mirrors have a long association with superstition and mythology. The Greek god Narcissus fell in love with and grew sick over his own reflection in a pool of water. An ancient Chinese myth tells of the Fauna of Mirrors, an alternative reality filled with monsters and demons. And people still whisper that if you look in a mirror on New Year's Eve and speak aloud the name of a dead person, they'll appear before you.

Look in the uppermost corners of most stores and you might see mirrors. These convex mirrors are used to deter shoplifters and other potential criminals. How does this mirror differ from other mirrors?

There are three types of mirror. Plane mirrors are similar to the ones in your bathroom. Concave mirrors are the ones found in makeup mirrors, and convex mirrors are often found on the passenger side of a car or in stores. Each one interacts with light in different ways.

A plane mirror, such as the one in your bathroom, is a sheet of glass with a silvery smooth coating on the back. Light passes through the glass and hits the smooth coating. The light is reflected off the coating and comes back toward you. The reflection creates an image of the object in front of the mirror. This is a copy of what the object looks like. The image is a virtual image; it's the same size as the original object and faces in the same direction (when you look in the mirror your head is up, unless you are doing a handstand). But there is something a little off.

VIRTUAL IMAGE

Look in a plane mirror. Wave to your reflection using your right hand. What do you see in the mirror? It looks as if your left hand is moving, correct? Right and left in a plane mirror are reversed.

LIGHT RAYS

When talking about convex or concave mirrors, it is important to have an understanding about light rays. There are two important terms to know.

- Optical axis—this is a line (an imaginary line) that divides a mirror in half.

- Focal point—this is a point (again, an imaginary point) where all those reflected light rays meet.

The image you see when you look in a concave mirror all depends on where the image is with respect to the focal point. If the object is far away from the focal point, then the object will be smaller and upside down. This upside down image is referred to as a real image. It is called real because this is where the actual reflected rays meet.

⚛ **Depending on where you stand in relation to the focal point of a mirror, your reflection will appear upside down and small, upside down and large, right side up and large, right side up and small, or it won't appear at all.**

REAL IMAGE

OH, WOW!

LIGHT RAYS

OPTICAL AXIS   F

FOCAL POINT

FOCAL LENGTH

CONCAVE MIRROR

If the object is beyond the focal point, but close to it, then the image will be real (upside down, remember) and big. If an object is placed between the mirror's surface and the focal point, then the image will be a virtual image and larger than the real object. A virtual image is right side up.

If an object is placed directly at the focal point of a concave mirror, there will be no image. This might be useful to aspiring shoplifters or vampires. However, it's very difficult to know exactly where the focal point is, so it's a good idea to have a backup plan.

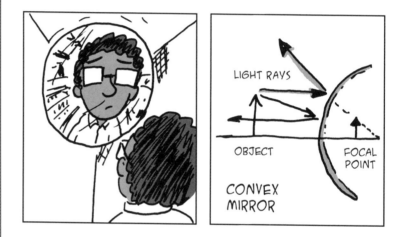

CONVEX MIRROR

Convex mirrors curve outward. Besides hanging in the corners of stores, convex mirrors are also found on the passenger side of cars. Look closely at one of those and you might see some form of the phrase, "Objects in mirror are closer than they appear." How is that possible? It has to do with the way light strikes the mirror's surface.

The focal point in this type of mirror is always behind it. This means that the light rays will never meet, as is shown in the diagram. The image created will always, no matter where the image is with respect to the mirror, be virtual and smaller.

⚛ Ships are warned by lighthouses to stay away from dangerous rocky shores. Now lighthouses are electrified, but they used to rely on candlelight. In 1822, Augustin Fresnel invented a lens that magnified the lighthouse flame so that ships even 20 miles away could see it. The Fresnel lens looks like a giant beehive and is designed to refract the light into a narrow, concentrated beam.

REFRACTION

Sometimes light rays bend, or refract. This happens as light passes from one medium, or substance, to another.

Fill a clear glass with water. Place a pencil in the glass and notice how the pencil appears to bend. See how that bend appears at the boundary between the air and the water in the glass? This is refraction. As the light passes from a less-dense medium—the air—to a denser medium—the water—the light rays slow down and bend.

LENSES

Cameras, binoculars, eyeglasses, and contact lenses are all designed to bend or refract light. Each of these contains one or more lenses. A lens is a piece of glass, or some other transparent material, used to do this.

A stroll around the mall will show many different types of lenses for sale. If you enter a science store or a toy store, you might find magnifying glasses on display. Pick one up and look through it at a small object. What do you see? The object is magnified—it looks larger than it is. This magnifying glass is a convex lens.

A convex lens is thicker in the center than it is on the edges. Light that enters into the lens bends toward the center. Lenses have focal points, just like mirrors. If an object is placed beyond the focal point of the lens, a real image forms. If the object is placed between the lens and the focal point, a virtual image forms.

A concave lens is thinner in the center than on the edges. The light rays that pass through a concave lens bend away and never meet. These lenses only create virtual images. The virtual image is always smaller than the actual object and right side up.

Inquire & Investigate ▶

A MATTER OF SECURITY

Security personnel at the mall believe that new surveillance equipment will help decrease rates of shoplifting. They want a device that can be used behind a post or counter while still providing a good look at the entire store. Design a device that can be both secret and useful.

🔬 VOCAB LAB

Write down what you think each word means: **transparent**, **translucent**, **opaque**, **concave**, **convex**, **virtual image**, **light rays**, and **refract**. Compare your definitions with those of your friends or classmates. Did you all come up with the same meanings? Turn to the text and glossary if you need help.

- **Start by mapping out the scene.** If a security guard wants to be able to remain hidden behind a post but needs to see the counter where all the candy and magazines are displayed, what angles and distances need to be considered?

- **Create a map that traces how an image of the counter could reach your eyes behind the post.** Is it better for security to have a handheld device or should the viewing apparatus be installed at the counter? Will mirrors or lenses be most useful in this situation, or some combination of the two? Should those mirrors and lenses be concave, convex, or plane?

- **Create a detailed drawing of your new device.** Include arrows and image orientation of what the security guard will see. Be sure to label the lenses and mirrors and the light rays as they hit it.

To investigate more, build your device. Is it more like a periscope or like a series of mirrors mounted on the wall? Set up a scenario to test the effectiveness of the device. How well does it work? Were you able to see what was happening?

Ideas for Supplies ▼

- small concave lenses and mirrors
- small convex lenses and mirrors
- small plane mirrors
- empty paper towel tubes
- scissors
- string
- flashlight
- masking or duct tape

NEARSIGHTED OR FARSIGHTED?

Do you wear glasses or contact lenses? If you do, you might be nearsighted, which means you have difficulty seeing objects that are far away. Or you might be farsighted, which means you can see things that are far away but have difficulty seeing things up close. Concave lenses are used to correct nearsightedness.

Ideas for Supplies ▼

- convex mirror (actual side mirror from a car or bike would be best)
- materials to mount the mirror
- paper
- measuring tape
- timer
- solid structure, such as a bookcase or door

HEY! WHERE DID IT GO! I CAN'T SEE IT ANYMORE.

BLIND SPOT

It's hard to believe, but at certain times a large car, truck, or SUV may actually disappear from your view. The blind spot is one of the greatest hazards of driving. Rearview mirrors are only helpful when a car is not in your blind spot. With the following experiment, you'll learn more about blind spots and discover ways to minimize them.

- **Mount the convex mirror onto a solid vertical surface.** A bookcase or a door is a good place to do this. Your mirror will simulate the side mirror on a car. Be sure that you can see behind you in the mirror.

- **With a group of friends, work to find the blind spot in your mirror.** Record your observations in your science journal. Consider several factors:

  - the size of the object in the blind spot,
  - when the object comes into sight and when it disappears, and
  - how long the object stays in the blind spot.

To investigate more, move your mirror in order to eliminate the blind spot as much as possible. Consider adding other mirrors—concave, convex, or plane—to the mirror you have in order to increase visibility. What changes could you make that would increase driving safety?

DECONSTRUCTING A RAINBOW

◀ **Inquire & Investigate**

Red, orange, indigo, and violet—and all the colors in between. Rainbows are beautiful phenomena formed as sunlight passes through raindrops in the sky and is refracted into the different colors of the visible spectrum. In this experiment, you will discover how to make a rainbow, and then how to take it apart, one color at a time.

Ideas for Supplies ▼

- prism
- white construction paper
- flashlight or lamp
- colored pencils
- small cardboard with thin slits cut into it

- **Use the prism, the flashlight, and the white piece of paper to create a rainbow.** Use colored pencils to trace the different bands of colors.

- **Use the cardboard with the slits to see if you can separate the different colors of the rainbow.** Consider the following:

    - is it as easy to isolate the red as it is to isolate the violet?

    - how wide should the slit be to get each color by itself?

    - is each color distinct or is there some bleeding of the colors?

> To investigate more, set up another prism and see what happens when the two rainbows coincide. Are you still able to separate the individual bands of color? What happens if the red band from one prism is crossed with the blue band of the other prism? What colors can you make?

THE EYES HAVE IT!

Your eyes can play tricks on you. Check out these optical illusions and see if you can train yourself to see through the illusion!

Chapter 8 ▶
Sound

Why can you hear
sounds even when
you can't see the
source of the sound?

⚛ Sound waves can bend around corners, move though solids, liquids, and gases, and travel long distances to reach your ear. Sound can't travel where there's no medium to travel through. That's why it's silent in space!

Chloe is walking her dog, Zeke, in the park on a bright and sunny day. The birds sing, a group of 10-year-olds practices soccer in a nearby field, a quartet rehearses a concert in the outdoor amphitheater, taxis, buses, and cars drive slowly along the street, stopping at the red light and occasionally honking their horns. A traffic officer directs traffic using a whistle. Zeke responds to Chloe's dog whistle. Suddenly an ambulance rushes by and drowns out all the other noise—then all goes relatively quiet again.

This scene is full of physics—the physics of sound. Sound is actually a series of waves caused by some sort of disturbance. Think of that disturbance as a vibration. Imagine a guitar string. When plucked, the string vibrates. The vibrations in the string disturb the air molecules closest to it. The air molecules compress together and then spread apart. This creates a wave.

Sound can travel through many different media. It can travel through the air, as Chloe found when she heard the sirens, yelling children, and dogs barking in the park. Anyone who has heard someone knocking on a door knows that sound can travel through a solid. And perhaps you have been at a local pool or pond and have tried to talk to your friend while underwater. It works, but it's not easy to understand exactly what's being said. Sound can travel through a liquid as well.

As Chloe walks through the park, she notices that the soccer team's shouts and hollers are echoing slightly. You have probably heard an echo before, in a cave, tunnel, empty room, across a canyon, or in a park like the one Chloe is in. Echoes occur when sound waves hit a surface and bounce back. The sound waves are reflected. These sound waves from the shouting soccer players hit the hard surface of the wall and bounce back to Chloe's ears. There is a delay between the time the sound is made and the moment it reaches her ears. The result is a hollow sort of noise, which may repeat. A very clear echo may sound like "Hello, hello, hello."

SUPER-FAST

On October 14, 1947, Chuck Yeager became the first person ever to fly a plane faster than the speed of sound. To do this, he flew his plane at more than 39,000 feet (12,000 meters) in altitude, because it's much colder up there! At the altitude he was flying, the temperature was about -74 degrees Fahrenheit (-59 degrees Celsius). Sound only travels at a speed of about 961 feet per second (293 meters per second) at that temperature. So he was able to travel faster than sound there by pushing his plane to speeds of 1,024 feet per second (312 meters per second).

PHYSICS FACT

Sound is a longitudinal wave. The energy moves through a medium parallel to the direction the wave travels. This is opposed to transverse waves, which move across the direction of wave movement, or perpendicular to it.

⚛ **What kind of setting makes for the best echoes? Visit this site to hear some examples of echoes.**

Chloe walks Zeke to the top of a hill. She is surprised that she can hear the noises from so far away. In fact, she notices that the traffic policeman and his whistle are actually behind the stone wall that surrounds the park. The only opening on that side of the wall is a large doorway placed far from where the traffic officer stands. Chloe wonders how she can still hear the whistle, even when she does not have a direct line of sight of the policeman.

This is possible because of another property of sound—diffraction. Sound waves do not travel in straight paths. They can bend around corners and through openings.

PHYSICS FACT

Did you know you can "feel" sound waves as well? Put your hand on top of a piano while someone is playing, or on a guitar as it is being strummed. Or even put your hand on your throat and hum. You are feeling vibrations—sound waves.

On her walk, Chloe notices something else as well. As she pauses a while to throw the ball to Zeke, she notices that the sounds she hears—the traffic, the siren, the shouts of the kids, the birds—all reach her at the same time. Some sources of the sound are farther away while others are closer to her, but there is no delay to the sounds reaching her ears.

The speed of sound depends on the temperature and the material through which the sound is traveling. For example, at 68 degrees Fahrenheit (20 degrees Celsius), sound travels through air at 1,125 feet per second (343 meters per second). But at 32 degrees Fahrenheit (0 degrees Celsius), the speed of sound is about 1,083 feet per second (330 meters per second). That doesn't seem like a big difference, but it is!

CAN YOU HEAR ME NOW?

One of the first things that many people think about in connection to sound is the idea of loudness. Is the sound loud or soft? Is it a whisper you need to strain to hear? Or is it loud enough to hurt your ears? Loudness is measured in decibels (dB). Sounds greater than 100 decibels can cause hearing damage over long periods of time.

Loudness is actually a subjective property of sound— it is how one individual perceives the energy of sound waves. Generally, the closer you are to a sound, the louder it is. So, it makes sense that the loudness of a sound depends on the amount of energy released and the distance from the source of a sound.

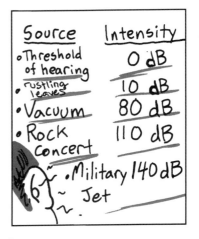

Source	Intensity
○ Threshold of hearing	0 dB
• rustling leaves	10 dB
• Vacuum	80 dB
• Rock Concert	110 dB
• Military Jet	140 dB

PITCH

Back at the park, an ambulance suddenly speeds down the road, followed closely by a fire truck and police car. The sirens are blaring the whole way. Chloe notices that the sound from the siren changes as it approaches and passes her. It is the pitch of the sound that changes. Pitch is a description of how a sound sounds. A bird tweeting in a tree might have a high pitch. Other sounds have a low pitch. A barking bulldog might have a low pitch. The pitch of a sound is determined by the frequency of the sound waves.

☀ **Visit this site to hear an example of the Doppler effect.**

THE SPEED OF SOUND

Some airplanes can travel very close to the speed of sound. When this happens, the sound waves pile up in front of the plane. When the plane then increases speed and goes faster than the speed of sound, it has to push its way through those piled-up sound waves. The sound waves overlap and release a tremendous amount of energy. The result? A sonic boom.

The fire truck or police car siren is sending out sound waves. As the siren approaches Chloe, the waves have to travel a shorter distance to reach her ears. Each wave takes less time to reach her than the previous one. The frequency with which the waves reach her increases, and she hears a higher-pitched noise. As it passes her by and continues down the road, the distance the waves have to travel to reach her increases, which lowers the frequency of the waves. The pitch decreases. But to the firefighters in the truck, the pitch stays the same. They are moving with the siren itself and the distance between their ears and the source of the noise does not change. This is known as the Doppler effect. It describes the change in the frequency of a wave as the source of the sound moves with respect to the listener.

MUSIC

No discussion of sound would be complete without a mention of music. Music is the arrangement of notes in a way that is pleasing to listen to. This is opposed to noise, which is a sound that can be unpleasant and has no musical patterns.

As Chloe and Zeke finish their walk, they stop to listen to the street musicians. One woman plays a guitar and sings while another man plays the bongos.

What makes some sounds musical and others noisy? Why does some music make us feel like dancing while other music makes us sleepy? Why does some music make us feel happy and other music make us feel sad? Humans have been debating the answers to these questions for hundreds of years. When played, musical instruments produce sound waves. One type of sound wave is a standing wave, which occurs at a certain frequency called the natural frequency. Every object has its own unique natural frequencies.

The lowest natural frequency of a standing wave is called the fundamental tone. The higher natural frequencies are called overtones. The note you hear played on a musical instrument is determined by the fundamental tone. For example, a musician may play a middle C on both a trumpet and a piano. Those notes have the same fundamental tone. But each instrument has different overtones which makes the note sound different.

The quality of a sound is also affected by resonance. Resonance is what happens when one object causes a nearby object to vibrate at its natural frequency. Resonance can increase the loudness of some overtones. This explains why a guitar is shaped the way it is, with the strings stretched over the open hole and hollow body. Its shape helps determine which overtones are loudest.

And finally, it's the surroundings that give a sound one last quality. Think about how a song may sound different in the shower or in a car than it does in an open room or gymnasium. These differences are the result of acoustics—how sound interacts with its surroundings. Sound waves may interfere with each other. They can distort the sound or even create an area where the loudness is decreased significantly. Concert halls and amphitheaters are designed to control the acoustics of sound.

FEELIN' GOOD

Our emotional response to music—how it can make us feel different things—has never been fully explained. Using MRI scans, scientists have proved that listening to music releases dopamine in our brains, which makes us feel good in the same way food makes us feel good. But is music necessary for our survival? Maybe! Can you think of ways music might help us in evolutionary terms?

THE SHAPE OF THE GUITAR DETERMINES RESONANCE.

THE PHYSICS OF SOUND COMES TO LIFE IN MY ACOUSTIC GUITAR.

SO THE SOUND WILL SOUND AMAZING!

LET'S PLAY "BLINDFOLD–AND LISTEN–AND GO SEEK"

Quite often, the distance from a sound makes a big difference in how it sounds to your ears. Someone knocking at your front door sounds very different if you are in a distant room compared to when you are right next to the door. The type of object making a sound determines how you perceive the noise as well. Someone knocking on your door with his or her fist sounds significantly less loud than someone using the heavy, metal doorknocker.

- **You and a partner can play a game of "blindfold—and listen—and go seek" to discover how distance and material type affect sound.**

- **Decide which partner will be blindfolded.** The other partner will choose an object from the table.

- **Position yourselves in different parts of the room.** The person who will be dropping the objects should be in the middle of the room. The person with the blindfold should be near one end of the room. The blindfolded partner should listen very carefully to determine where each object lands after it is tossed.

- **Gently and carefully, toss an object to a distant corner of the room.** Take care not to hit anything with the object. Also try to do this so that the object does not slide or roll too far.

- **The person who is blindfolded should walk toward the sound, trying to locate the object.** Once you think you are near it, remove your blindfold and see if you are correct.

> To investigate more, repeat several times with different objects. Be sure to try out large objects and smaller objects, objects made of soft material and those made of harder material. What differences do you discover? Do you notice a pattern? What does this say about sound and the material making the sound?

Ideas for Supplies ▼

- an empty, quiet room
- several objects, both hard and soft, such as a pen, pencil, dice, banana, cloth napkin
- blindfold

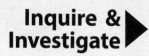
ARE YOU MUSICAL?

Musical instruments have been around for thousands of years. Long ago, people made instruments from very simple materials, such as rocks and sticks. You yourself probably made music by banging on pots and pans with a wooden spoon when you were younger.

The sound an instrument makes depends on many factors. Given a few simple objects, can you make an instrument that sounds good to the ear?

ACOUSTICS AND SCIENCE

There are several scientific disciplines that utilize the science of acoustics. For example, bioacoustics is the study of the use of sound by animals such as dolphins or bats. Biomedical acoustics uses sound in medicine, as in the case of ultrasound technology. And psychoacoustics is the study of how people react to sound.

Ideas for Supplies ▼

- rubber bands
- paper towel or toilet paper rolls
- string
- plastic bottles
- cardboard boxes
- dowels or wooden spoons
- plastic pipes

- **Decide what type of instrument you want to make.** Will it be something you hit, pluck, strum, or blow into or across? Gather your materials. You will also need to decide how you will manipulate the materials to change the pitch.

- **Design your instrument on paper first.** Create a detailed drawing of your proposed instrument. Be sure to include predictions about the pitch and how it can be changed. Additionally, provide a set of instructions on how to use the instrument.

- **Build it! Using your materials, build your instrument.** Test it by playing a simple tune. Make any modifications you might need.

To investigate more, work with friends or classmates to develop a unique sound or song using several different homemade instruments. Try your music in different locations such as the hallway, the auditorium, and outside. Which sounds best? Determine how to use all the instruments in order to create the most pleasing and interesting sounds. Prepare a concert for family and friends.

THAT'S TOO LOUD!

Noise pollution is a real thing. It is the result of excessive noises that impact everyday life or health. Perhaps you are exposed to noise pollution. Construction noise, traffic, machinery, or excessive music can all be considered noise pollution.

Some noise pollution is merely a nuisance. It may prevent you from concentrating on your homework or from getting a good night's sleep. Other noise pollution can harm your ears and lead to hearing loss. This experiment will show how some soundproofing materials can significantly reduce noise pollution.

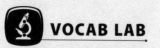

VOCAB LAB

Write down what you think each word means: **vibration, diffraction, loudness, decibels, pitch, medium, fundamental tone,** and **resonance.** Compare your definitions with those of your friends or classmates. Did you all come up with the same meanings? Turn to the text and glossary if you need help.

- **Work with a partner to determine a reasonable loudness on the MP3 player.** Record the decibel reading using the sound meter.

- **Develop a procedure to test the perceived loudness from different distances.** Use materials at your disposal. Be sure to create a well-developed procedure that other people can follow.

- **Design your protective device.** Things to consider:

  - the comfort of the device,

  - the ease with which it can be used,

  - how well it blocks the noise, and

  - safety.

- **Test your device.** Have your partner repeat the same steps that he or she did previously, listening to noises from certain distances. What is your partner's perception of the sound at each distance?

To investigate more, visit places that can be loud, such as a train station, auditorium, or school bus. How can you improve your protective device so it works in places like these? How can you alter the design to make the device subtle to use? Why is it important for people to be able to control the level of sound they are exposed to? Is the world getting louder or quieter with time? What do you think your town sounded like a hundred years ago? Two hundred years ago?

✳ If a tree falls in the forest and no one is there to hear it, does it make a sound? Yes, if you are measuring volume: The fall produces measurable sound waves that have volume. No, if you are measuring loudness, which depends on someone being there to hear the crash.

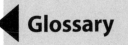

A

acceleration: a change in velocity, expressed as a rate.

acoustics: the study of how sound interacts with its surroundings.

action force: the force created by one object that acts upon another.

air resistance: an example of fluid friction that occurs as objects fall through the air.

ammeter: a device used to measure current.

ampere: the basic unit of electrical current.

atom: the smallest particle from which all elements are made.

atomic number: the number of protons in the nucleus of an atom.

atomic weight: the average weight of an atom in an element.

average speed: the speed at which an object moves overall. To calculate average speed, divide the total distance the object travels by the total time.

B

balanced force: when forces that are equal act in opposite directions on an object.

battery: two or more electrochemical cells, arranged in a series.

C

circuit: the path a current takes.

color: a quality perceived by humans that can be described using words such as red, blue, green, and yellow.

combined force: when two or more forces work together.

concave lens: a lens that is thicker at the edges than at the center.

concave mirror: a mirror that curves inward.

concept: a general idea or principle that determines how we understand nature.

conduction: the transfer of electrons by contact between two objects.

conductor: any material that an electric charge can easily flow through. Said to conduct heat well.

convex mirror: a mirror that curves outward.

D

deceleration: a negative acceleration, or decrease in speed.

decibel: a unit of measurement of loudness.

diffraction: the bending of a wave (sound waves included) as it moves around something or through an opening.

Doppler effect: a change in the frequency of waves that occurs as an object changes position with respect to an observer.

E

echo: a reflected sound wave.

electric current: the flow of electric charges.

electric field: the area around a charged object.

electric force: a description of the amount of attraction or repulsion between electric charges.

electrochemical cell: a device that changes chemical energy into electrical energy.

electrode: a conductor used to make contact with the nonmetallic part of a circuit.

Glossary ▶

electrolyte: a compound found within an electrochemical cell. Electrodes are suspended in an electrolyte.

electron spin: the motion of electrons around a nucleus.

electron: a negatively charged particle swirling around the nucleus of an atom.

electroscope: a device that is able to detect electric charges.

element: a pure substance that can't be broken down.

energy: the ability or power to do things, to work.

estimation: an opinion or guess about something.

F

ferromagnetic: a property of certain elements (including iron) to form permanent magnets.

fluid friction: the friction resulting when an object moves through a fluid, such as air or water.

fluid: a liquid or a gas.

focal point: the point where light rays meet (or seem to meet) after being reflected from a mirror or lens.

force: a push or pull that changes the speed or direction of an object.

formula: a rule that is expressed by symbols and numbers.

free fall: an object falling when only gravity is working on it, not friction.

friction: the force that resists motion between two objects in contact.

fundamental tone: the lowest natural frequency of an object.

fundamental: basic or central.

G

gravitational pull: the pull of gravity on an object.

gravity: a force that pulls objects toward each other, and all objects to the earth.

ground: a wire in a house or building that is connected to the earth's surface (or ground).

grounded: a circuit in which the current flows directly into the ground.

I

image: a copy of an object created by refraction or reflection.

induction: the movement of electrons from one part of an object to another part of the same object.

inertia: the tendency of an object to resist a change in motion. An object in motion tends to stay in motion and an object at rest tends to stay at rest.

instantaneous speed: the speed of an object at one specific point in time.

insulator: a material through which electric charges cannot flow. An insulator doesn't conduct heat well.

interaction: how things work together.

isolation: separate and by itself.

L

lab: short for laboratory, a place where scientific research is done.

law of conservation of charge: the idea that charges cannot be created or destroyed.

law of conservation of momentum: the idea that the total momentum of objects that interact does not change unless acted upon by an outside force.

lens: a piece of glass that is curved and refracts light.

longitudinal wave: a wave that moves in the direction parallel to the direction that the wave is traveling.

loudness: the perception of sound.

M

magnet: any material that attracts iron or objects containing iron.

magnetic domain: an area in which all the magnetic fields of atoms are aligned.

magnetic field: an area around a magnet where magnetic force is.

magnetic force: a force that occurs when the poles of a magnet interact.

magnetic pole: the ends of a magnet, either north or south, where the magnetic force is the strongest.

mass: the amount of matter in an object.

matter: anything that takes up space and has mass.

momentum: the product of the mass and velocity of an object.

motion: when the distance between two or more objects is changing.

music: tones and overtones that are pleasing to listen to.

N

negative acceleration: deceleration, or a decrease in speed of an object in motion.

net force: the sum total of all combined forces.

neutron: a particle found within some nuclei that has no charge.

newton: a unit of measure of force. It is the force required to move 1 kilogram at 1 kilometer per second squared.

Newton's first law of motion: an object at rest remains at rest and an object in motion stays in motion unless acted upon by an outside force.

Newton's second law of motion: acceleration is directly proportional to the force on an object and inversely proportional to the mass of that object.

Newton's third law of motion: for every action, there is an equal but opposite reaction.

nucleus: the center of an atom containing protons and neutrons.

O

Ohm's law: resistance is equal to voltage divided by current.

opaque: a material that either reflects or absorbs all the light that strikes it.

optical axis: an imaginary line that divides a mirror in half.

overtone: a natural frequency that is a multiple of the frequency of the fundamental tone.

P

parallel circuit: an electric circuit with a number of different paths.

periodic table: a list that shows the chemical elements arranged according to their properties.

permanent magnet: a magnet containing material that keeps its magnetism.

Glossary ▶

phenomenon: something seen or observed. Plural is phenomena.

philosopher: someone who thinks about and questions the way things are in the world.

physicist: a scientist who studies energy and matter.

physics: the study of physical forces, including matter, energy, and motion, and how these forces interact with each other.

pitch: the perception of the frequency of a sound.

plane mirror: a flat mirror that produces an image that is upright, virtual, and the same size as the original object.

point of reference: a location or an object to compare to when determining if an object is in motion.

potential difference: what causes electric circuits to flow.

practical: something useful in everyday situations.

principle: an important idea or assumption that a system of thought is based on.

probability: the likelihood that something will happen.

projectile motion: the path that a projectile takes as it travels.

projectile: an object that is thrown.

property: a characteristic quality or distinctive feature of something.

proton: a positively charged particle within the nucleus of an atom.

R

ramp: a sloping surface.

real image: an upside-down image formed in a mirror.

reflection: when an object (such as a ball) or a wave (such as a sound or light wave) bounces back when it hits an object through which it can't pass.

refraction: when a wave bends as it passes from one medium to a different medium.

repel: push away.

resistance: a force that opposes or slows down another force.

resonance: an increase in amplitude in order to match the natural frequency of an object.

rolling friction: the friction that happens when an object such as a wheel rolls over a surface.

S

science: the study of the physical and natural world, using observation.

series circuit: an electrical circuit with only one path.

short circuit: a situation in which a current takes the path of least resistance. It may result in an electric shock.

simple cell: what we think of (and buy in the store) as batteries.

sliding friction: the friction between two objects when one object slides across another object.

slope: the steepness of a line, measured as rise divided by run.

sound: a series of waves caused by some sort of disturbance.

speed: the distance an object travels in a unit of time.

standing wave: what appears to be a wave not moving that is actually two waves that are interfering with each other.

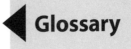

static discharge: the loss of static electricity.

static electricity: a buildup of electric charges on an object.

static friction: the friction between two objects that are not in motion relative to each other.

stationary: not moving.

streamlined: a design with a smooth surface that minimizes resistance through air or water.

T

temporary magnet: a magnet made of material that loses its magnetism.

terminal velocity: the greatest velocity a falling object reaches.

terminal: the points on a battery where electricity enters or leaves, or the portion of the electrode that sticks up out of the electrolyte.

texture: a rough surface.

theoretical: a set of facts and principles used to explain phenomena, especially in science.

third prong: the part of an electric plug that provides an alternate path for the circuit to flow. The third prong is a safety measure.

translucent: a description of matter that scatters the light rays that pass through it.

transparent: a description of matter that allows light rays to pass through it.

transverse wave: a wave that moves perpendicular to the direction in which the wave is moving.

turbulence: violent movements in a fluid, such as air or water.

U

unbalanced force: when forces that are unequal work to move an object.

V

variable: the part of the experiment that is able to be changed.

velocity: the speed of an object in a particular direction.

virtual image: an image in a mirror that is upright.

volt: the unit used to measure the electric potential between two spots in a circuit.

voltage: the electrical potential or energy difference between two spots in a circuit.

voltmeter: a device used to measure voltage.

W

weight: the force of gravity on an object.

CHECK IT OUT! I'M MAKING TRANSVERSE WAVES!

BOOKS

Isaac Newton and Physics for Kids: His Life and Ideas with 21 Activities
Kerrie Logan Hollihan, Chicago Review Press, 2009

Physics I For Dummies
Steven Holzner, For Dummies, 2011

Mad About Physics: Braintwisters, Paradoxes, and Curiosities
Christopher Jargodzki and Franklin Potter, Wiley, 2000

Albert Einstein and Relativity for Kids: His Life and Ideas with 21 Activities and Thought Experiments
Jerome Pohlen, Chicago Review Press, 2012

WEB SITES

Golems–Design your own machine and watch it work here at this website.
golemgame.com

Physics for Kids–All you want to know about physics . . . and a little bit more.
scienceforkids.kidipede.com/physics

The Exploratorium: Ear Guitar–Learn to build and play an ear guitar.
exploratorium.edu/science_explorer/ear_guitar.html

NOVA: Special Effects in the Movies–Find out the physics behind some of your favorite special effects!
pbs.org/wgbh/nova/specialfx/fxguide/fxuemmm.html

The Exploratorium: Skateboard Science–Take a closer look at the physics of skateboarding.
exploratorium.edu/skateboarding

The Hubble Space Telescope–Check out these photos taken with the Hubble Telescope.
nasa.gov/mission_pages/hubble/multimedia/index.html

Watch, Know, and Learn–Watch this video to "see" sound waves!
watchknowlearn.org/Video.aspx?VideoID=37512&CategoryID=2548

The Wonders of Physics–Check out some of the videos and activities on this website.
sprott.physics.wisc.edu/wop.htm

Amaze your Friends–See what you can do with a balloon and some BBQ skewers.
physics.org/interact/physics-to-go/balloon-kebabs/index.html

Index

Index ▶

G

H

I

L

M

N

O

P